ZEHHU

Zehhu

Library of Congress Control Number: 2015943877

ISBN: 978-1-63308-153-6 Hardback
         978-1-63308-154-3 Paperback
         978-1-63308-155-0 Digital

Interior and Cover Design by R'tor John D. Maghuyop

CHALFANT ECKERT
PUBLISHING

1028 S Bishop Avenue, Dept. 178
Rolla, MO 65401

Printed in United States of America

CROSSING
THE BRIDGE
FROM
DEPRESSION
TO LIFE

ZEHHU

BEN ISAAC

CHALFANT ECKERT
PUBLISHING

The purpose of this book is to provide simple, effective,

and practical strategies to those who are struggling with depression.

All characters in this book are fictitious. Any resemblance to real

persons, living or not, is purely coincidental.

To Aliyah

TABLE OF CONTENTS

INTRODUCTION

You are now in a major battle for your own survival. If you allow the flood waters of depression to drown you, all may be lost, even your own life. I am telling you today what I wish someone had told me twelve years ago when I was going through one of the darkest periods in my life. You may save yourself countless hours of sadness if you are able to apply some of the ideas that I present in this book.

While there is no known cure for depression[1], there are strategies that can be used to help someone, yourself or another, to deal more effectively with depression and find a way to take part in life once again.

Even the first utterance of the word *Zehhu*[2], meaning "to stop descending into deeper depression," might be enough to pull a person out of a deep depression. I do not know all the details of your depression. All I know is that you are there and looking for answers, looking for a way to stop the pain, get relief, and get back to living. If you keep going on the road you are now on, it will lead to a life with no joy or happiness or, even worse, a life where you just want out for good in order to escape the darkness of depression.

You might also be equipped to help someone that you care about who has fallen into depression. In either case, I am going to give you my best strategies for how to cope with depression.

---

1 http://www.healthyplace.com/depression/depression-treatment/
   stop-depression-can-you-cure-depression/
2 Zehhu means "'that's it, "this is it,'" or "'enough,'" which I refer to as part of
   a methodology of how to stop the spiral down to deeper depression and start
   getting out.

These strategies may shave days, months, years, even decades off the unhappy state that you find yourself in. Make no mistake about it, depression kills you, your happiness, career, family, friends, relationships, and those around you. Do you need more reasons to take up arms and get ready to battle depression?

Let me tell you the story of a man who wanted to fight but had little energy left from his decade-long battle with depression and how he successfully crossed the bridge from depression to life. Several years ago I was invited to a wedding in Jerusalem, and as I was walking down Jaffa Road, I recognized a man who I had not seen in over forty years. When I was a teenager, I had eaten at his home as a guest of his father. This man, Michael, resembled his father so much that I could see the image of his father's face in his own.

Michael had heard through the grapevine that I had my own struggle with depression, family estrangement, and obesity. He thought that I might be open to speaking with a childhood friend of his that I will call "Joseph," who had been battling depression for close to a decade.

Besides being clinically depressed, Joseph was over 275 pounds and Michael feared that Joseph would never recover. Michael and others had tried many times but did not know how to help Joseph get out of his depression.

I told Michael that I would give it my best shot but could offer no guarantee to totally eradicate Joseph's depression and obesity, which is difficult for anyone to deal with, especially after ten years.

I wanted to achieve some success by at least rendering the depression manageable enough that Joseph would become interested in rebuilding his mind, his body, and ultimately his life. As soon as I got back to my apartment in New York City, I gave Joseph a call as I had promised Michael.

Joseph was a man in his late forties, but he sounded like he had already reached 120. He sounded very weak. He told me his story. He got married, he got divorced, and his children became estranged from him. He could not cope with the loss of the relationship with his children and sank deeper and deeper into depression. He started to take antidepressants and experienced serious negative side effects that led to the loss of his career.

He rarely left his apartment while he continued to mourn over his losses, and it appeared that he was just waiting to die. He was listless, with no energy, and spoke like a person who had been beaten to a pulp. A good part of the beatings were by him. I did my best to motivate him. I gave him the same strategies that I am sharing with you. I called him frequently and encouraged him as best as I could.

Since he had significant side effects from some of his medications, I followed up to see if he was able to do even the smallest of actions like taking a walk every day to get out of his apartment, to get moving physically, so that he could get healthier physically and even imagine himself moving past his problems conceptually. Joseph told me that he liked the ideas we were discussing and wanted to put them into practice, but then he would just say at the end of every sentence, "I don't know. I don't know," with a heavy breath of exasperation.

He kept saying that it was too late, it had been over a decade, there was no hope, he was too tired, mentally and physically; maybe it was because of the side effects of his medications. And then he would go back to the story about loving and missing all that he had in his previous life, especially his kids and his job. Once he did that, he just wanted to get off the phone so he could sink deeper into his depression where he seemed to feel most comfortable and safe.

Finally, a few weeks later, Joseph thanked me for my time and said that he needed to reflect on our conversations and he would be back in touch with me sometime soon. "Sometime soon" sounded more like "sometime never." Weeks passed by and then several months went by and neither I nor Michael had heard from Joseph again. When Michael and I spoke about the situation he confided in me that he was fearful that Joseph would become another statistic who would lose the battle with depression, and he had good reason to worry.

Statistically, 800,000 to a million people die by suicide every year, making suicide the tenth leading cause of death worldwide. Suicide rates are higher in men than in women, with males three to four times more likely than females to kill themselves. There are an estimated ten to twenty million non-fatal attempted suicides every year. Attempts are more common in young people and females.[3]

Anyone who has dealt with a person with depression understands what it is like when you feel like you are walking on eggshells with an individual. You never know what you might say or not say that can cause the dam to break wide open and make things worse.

Michael said he felt responsible and felt that he could not rest until he at least knew that Joseph was okay. He also thought that just having me call Joseph was not enough; he believed I should have to go to Joseph and see if connecting on a more personal level would be more beneficial.

He mentioned that his other friends had not seen Joseph for over a month, and no one could get in touch with him.

The first time I met Joseph, I was pretty shocked. Joseph looked listless and very pale and what I can best describe as catatonic[4]. He barely talked or moved. I did not know if his lack of movement was a result of depression or his meds. Before Joseph was divorced, he lived in a colonial-style home that he designed on an acre of land. The apartment he lived in now was barely 300 square feet, and his bed was right next to his five-foot-long "kitchen." There was little other furniture in his room, his clothing was strewn around the floor, and there was a pile of dishes in the sink.

---

3   http://en.wikipedia.org/wiki/Suicide

4   Of, relating to, being, resembling, or affected by a marked psychomotor disturbance that may involve stupor or mutism, negativism, rigidity, purposeless excitement, and inappropriate or bizarre posturing, also characterized by a marked lack of movement, activity, or expression.

I sat on the floor to speak with him as he had only one chair for himself. It was not a pleasant experience. It felt more like a hospital room than an apartment. All that was missing was Joseph wearing a white gown.

Joseph had a very hard time communicating. Nevertheless, I could see that he was glad that I was there, even though neither of us had much to say.

Over the course of time, we discussed the "prescription"[5] for a person to deal with depression with or without medication, as it had been determined that Joseph had treatment-resistant depression.

My sincere hope is that some or all of these ideas might be helpful to you or someone that you care about just as they were for Joseph and me. Thank you for not giving up. You have your life to live, so let's get started!

---

5   I am not a doctor, so I use the term *prescription* loosely, which is why I put it in quotes!

ZEHHU

The first time I spoke with Joseph was when I returned to New York City and gave him a call.

"Hello, Joseph, my name is Benjamin. I got your number and have greetings for you from Michael from Flushing, Queens. He said that he is a good friend of yours. He asked me to send you his best."

"Hello, Benjamin, yes, thanks. Michael? Wow, that brings back a lot of memories. Those were the good old days."

"He also told me that we share some common circumstances of divorce, estrangement, and depression. I struggle with a similar background as you. Michael thought that it might be good for both of us to speak to each other, perhaps we can be supportive of each other."

"Well, I am not sure that speaking about this…can help…it has only hurt me for the last decade since I lost my daughters…." And with that, his voice trailed off.

"Look, I do not mean to bring up any bad memories, but Michael thought that if we talk about some ideas of how to fight depression, it could be useful for both of us. I agreed to share the things I have done which have helped me and they could be helpful to you as well, plus you might have your own spin on how they can be made more effective and that can be helpful to me. Are you open to talking about it?"

"For Michael, I am willing to discuss anything. For me, I think it is too late. I am real tired, exhausted from lack of sleep, medications, and most of all, I am heartbroken over missing my daughters. I cannot live without them."

"I really do understand how painful family estrangements can be. I am not claiming that we can wipe away that reality or wave a magic wand and have it disappear, but I do think that there is another path that we can take. Let me start by telling you about a dream that I had a couple of years ago. Like you, I have been on antidepressants for depression. I have had my share of cocktails made up out of Zoloft, Prozac, and Effexor. I experienced side effects such as massive sweating at night to losing feeling in my lower legs. I also suffered from insomnia. I am not sure if that was caused by the meds or by nightmares I had."

"Oh yes, unfortunately, I can relate," Joseph said. "My medications have done a number on me as well. The worst of the side effects has been suicidal ideation and seeing my reflection in a mirror speaking when I was not saying anything. That really startled me. What did your doctors say about your reactions?"

"After several years of countless antidepressants and their negative side effects, they said that I have treatment-resistant depression and should look at alternative treatments like diet and/or exercise."

"Ah, maybe I have a similar situation," Joseph said. "So you were talking about a dream. What kind of dream, or was it a nightmare?"

"It was the same recurring nightmare. I was walking around in a house. I would see my kids but they would not see me or even notice me, no matter how much I waved or motioned to them. In every dream, I had no way to speak. I could not speak. I do not know why. At the end of the dream I would see a man standing in front of me in an elevator. I could not tell whether it was going up or down, but he appeared to be the person who operated the elevator. He was a bit rotund, older than me, grayer hair, and I wanted to ask him to get the elevator moving. Sometimes I thought that the man in the elevator was me years in the future. Before I could ask him, he seemed to sense that I wanted to speak with him, so he turned around. That was the point that I would wake up screaming because when he turned around, he had no mouth!"

"That would scare the living daylights out of me too."

"One day, " I continued, "I had another dream of not being visible to my children, even though I was standing right in front of them. I saw them running and playing but no matter where I was or what I did in the house, I was invisible. I heard their voices, but they did not hear mine. I saw them walking around, riding bicycles, but they did not see me. I wanted to scream and shout out to them. I wanted to call them, but again, it was as if I had no mouth, I had no words, I could not express myself, and I was not seen or heard. I struggled in the dream to speak but I could not move my mouth at all. The next thing I knew was that I was in the elevator again with the man in front of me. In every other dream like this for close to eight or nine years, I would wake up sweating, screaming and flailing my arms, but none of the words were coherent. I just sounded like Frankenstein when he realized he was on fire. This time, though, was different.

"When I woke up, I sat up to a sitting position on my bed and I was violently screaming a word that sounded like 'Zehhu.' I immediately knew that it meant enough, no more, I have had enough. I had to stop descending deeper and deeper into depression."

"You're right, that sure sounds like a terrible nightmare, a strange and scary dream."

"The best illustration I can give of how I felt coming out of the dream is Caesar in *Rise of the Planet of the Apes* dramatically screaming 'no' to the shock of the animal handler who was abusing him and everyone in the movie and the audience is just stunned. He is an ape and should not have the power of speech. Similarly, I never had the power of speech in my dreams. Finally I woke up in a sitting position shouting 'Zehhu.' What that meant to me was that there is a time to mourn and a time to rejoice. No matter how much we love our children, home, and job, we cannot mourn forever. There has to be a boundary. I think crying out 'Zehhu' was my subconscious message to myself, 'Enough! Stop the mourning. Start being productive. You have to take care of yourself because you cannot control how other people think or behave.' Plus, we do not know what is going on in their minds, so we cannot judge them. I am sure they have their own pain. No matter how many mistakes we have made, how long will we beat ourselves up over them? Can you say Zehhu, Joseph?"

"I never really thought about saying enough. I feel like I have been imprisoned and have no appeal and no exit out of my jail cell. I realize that even prisoners usually have a get out of jail date, unless it is for life. Did I do something that deserves life imprisonment and isolation? I know that I do not hold the key for me to get out of jail."

"Who holds the key?"

"My memories, my losses, my failures, and everything else that I am despondent about."

"So, unless you can change the past, you are going to stay locked up, in your own mental prison, for life?"

"Sounds crazy to do that, I admit that, it really sounds off the wall to give the past and present such power and to give me no power at all for my own freedom."

"Joseph, you also have a key, you also have a say in this matter. You are not in a physical prison, but you have been in a mental prison for so many years, trapped in your depression. Are you willing to use the keys that you have to release you from your mental jail cell? One of those keys is to say Zehhu. You have to tell yourself forcefully that you have had enough. I can tell you that for me, once I woke up shouting Zehhu, that was enough to stop the downward spiral. I had been sliding down deeper for years. I lost my career. I lost my home. I lost my marriage. I lost relationships with my children, friends, and family. If I did not stop, I had no boundary stopping me from going over a virtual or real cliff. Are you willing to say Zehhu?"

"I don't know. Let me think about it. The idea makes sense, but for some reason, I think that I still have to be sad, whether it is my mistakes or just the situation. How can I ever be happy?"

The first conversation that you must have with yourself in order to cross the bridge from depression to life is: "I am ready to say Zehhu. I am ready to say some word in any language that means 'I have had enough!'" Feel free to say it calmly, scream, shout, or cry out Zehhu! No matter what the source of your depression is, you should tell yourself that you are ready to declare Zehhu and at the very least, stop the downward spiral into deeper depression.

If you want to stop the momentum of your depression which is dragging down your life and the lives of those around you, then you have to say "Enough." At the bare minimum, you have to be willing to stop the slide into the pit of depression that leads nowhere, and produces nothing but bad feelings for everyone involved.

I understand that this is easier said than done, but that is my promise here, to give you strategies on how to cope with depression. I did not just say Zehhu, I screamed it at the top of my lungs. The primal scream that you have had enough of being mired in the bottomless pit can be your first step to freedom from the prison of depression.

If you are in a padded room or a forest where other people will not think you have gone totally mad, I would urge you to be passionate about it as well and scream out that you have had enough. "Zehhu, I have had enough!"

The same passion that you had in your depression, turn it around and use that same energy to bust out of it. Use that same dedication to negative energy, moping, sulking, and stressing to power your resolve to say with absolute certainty that you have had enough and that you are ready to change. If you were on a trip to Hawaii and discovered that you were on the wrong plane, and that you were actually on a flight to Oneonta, New York, you have to get off the plane and change course. You must stop, then change course so that you can get to your real destination.

No one wakes up one day and says, "You know, I am really looking forward to having a terrible day. I would even feel better if I sulk the entire day, wear a long face and frown, muster up as much bitterness as possible about the past, mourn as much as possible in the present, and fret and worry the rest of the time about the future which is scaring the daylights out of me." No one does that intentionally. I am sure that your depression is not the place where you really want to be. This state we call depression might cause your usual day to resemble something like the following. Upon waking up, your first thought is the last past memory or incident or event or current situation which is stressing you to no end. Your depressing thoughts continue from the previous night to the next morning when you wake up. That is why you do not want to wake up.

You are frightened that nothing ever seems to work out or that they will not work out.

You think of the people you have disappointed and those you think have disappointed you, people who have hurt you, whether they are friends or family, spouses or children, politicians or the local diner that really messed up your pancakes last Sunday.

Every person, thing, and event can be twisted to feed your depression. You are angry, you are bitter, you cannot believe your bad luck, you have no desire to do anything, you do not want to say anything, you cannot think of anything worthwhile to do other than remain in your room, on your bed or at your desk, or on the train, playing the scenes and conversations over and over in your head until they completely color your day from clear blue skies to battleship gray.

Even if it is a beautiful day, you will find a way to feel that it is a terrible day and wish that you had not been born. If the pain in your brain rises to the highest intensity, you will even think about ways to end the pain, even if it means taking your own life. You will start to imagine going to the top of a bridge or other methods which might be the most physically painless—or even painful—to stop the agonizing pain in your mind.

After revving yourself up to play the same video over and over again in your head, all the losses of your life, all the things that have gone wrong, you just spend the rest of the day in despair. You sit in your room of darkness, sometimes wanting no food, sometimes binging on junk food, sometimes using alcohol or drugs, but by the end of the day, you are just deeper in the pit. It is very difficult to get out of the pit of depression without a ladder, without someone to lend you a hand to pull you out. Once you sink down, it is really difficult to make it to stable ground. It is like quicksand, you just continue sinking. Is that how you want to spend the rest of your life? I asked Joseph that question.

"No, I don't, I honestly don't. I just don't know how to get out of this hole."

"Do you think that any of us really want to live that way? No matter what is the cause of our depression—whether it is endogenous depression caused by internal organic reasons, such as our biology, genes, hormones, or if it is exogenous depression caused by traumatic events such as war, crime, or tragedy—the bottom line is that we all have limited time on this planet and we do have the power to make different choices."

"Don't get so fancy with me here, Benjamin. What is this endogenous, exogenous stuff? Just give it to me straight with no dressing. Just give me an idea of how you think I can do things differently so that I can get out of this depression."

"This," I said, "is what I think your potential day could look like after first applying the fundamental idea of Zehhu."

NEW DAY AFTER ZEHHU

Upon waking up, your first thought is that you are grateful for opening your eyes, for being alive. You think about what you do have in your life. You think about what you would like to accomplish during the day, whether it be to complete a project, to help someone else out, to improve whatever you can in your life physically, financially, and spiritually, whatever it is that makes you feel stronger.

You know you have circumstances and experiences in your life that can cause the opposite, but you stay focused on what you can control. What are you happy about that you have right now? What excites you about the future? You keep your focus on the present and the future. You live with the satisfaction that you are going to give everything your best shot. You are confident things will work out in the future, the same way they have worked out in the past.

You are hopeful and expect that if you give it your all, you can make things happen in your life and see daily improvements. You do not live in fear. Nobody can be successful at whatever they are doing if they live in fear. You live with the awareness that you are accomplishing every moment and you are moving toward your goals. Instead of focusing on what might go wrong, you focus on your goals and that fuels your excitement in the day, especially when these goals are related to what you really love to do, whether art, music, accounting, medicine, or sports. Whatever it is that really makes you excited, that is where you should place your emphasis and work toward achieving those goals.

Think of the people in your life who have supported you. Think of those people who love you. Think of those people who care about you and be grateful for having them in your life.

Imagine being the person who cares about you when you are in your depressed state.

Imagine what life is like for them. Forget about you for a second, and imagine their life.

I remember sharing those thoughts with Joseph, and this was the response: "True, I never thought about that..."

I responded, "You bleed all over them, you repeat your stories ad infinitum, not only for days, but weeks, even years, perhaps for a whole lifetime, the same stories that you use to support being depressed. I am sure that you can imagine that it is no picnic for them. So, instead of flooding them with your negative energy, you appreciate these people, and show them that you care about them too.

"How about a smile? Instead of a frown, greet them with a smile. What about all the people you say have disappointed you or hurt you, whether friends or family, spouses or children, or, even politicians or the local diner if they really messed up your pancakes last Sunday?

"Let them be and let your emotional frustrations go. You cannot control their thoughts or actions. Stop giving them so much space in your mind that you cannot enjoy the people that are in front of you and want to be in your life, including yourself! Give yourself precedence and do what is good for you. You feel good; count your good fortune no matter how trivial you think it might be. You can see, great, you can hear, wonderful, you have the use of your body and it is working despite how much abuse you have meted out to it, awesome. Living is a matter of perspective.

"You do have a lot to be thankful for and you have to recognize it. You want to make an effort to increase your good fortune. Nobody throws money in the bank hoping that it will decrease. Everyone puts their money in the bank hoping it will yield an increase.

"You get up and get started on your day, working toward your goals. Even if it is rainy outside, you are still going to have a great day. Even if the sky is battleship gray, it will be as if there are clear blue skies. When you do speak, you will be speaking of good things, your goals, and what you appreciate. You will get outside to enjoy the day, the air, take a walk, work out, live the healthiest lifestyle possible, because you do have a desire to be creative and accomplish your goals, whatever they may be.

"When you do think of the past, you think of your past accomplishments. They are proof that you can be successful once you put your mind to it. Even during the cold of winter, if you are following your path, you will be thankful that you were born; that you received the gift of life and you will do your best to make the most of it. You will be free of the pain of failure in your mind.

"There are always challenges, but the pain is gone. Instead, you are content with where you are right now and you want to keep improving in every way possible. Imagine new ways of celebrating your life and the ones that you love, and number one must be yourself.

"This mindset is not selfish, but realistic, because if you do not care about yourself, or your own happiness, who can trust you to care about their happiness? Think of places that you might want to go to celebrate all the good in your life. You might want to take a vacation to Italy, maybe purchase a new home, get a different career, help out others, whatever it is, you will be thinking of climbing to the top of your Mount Everest, or whatever your big challenges are, and you are climbing up there, not to jump off, but to raise your arms in victory that you have made it. You can beat the mountain of your own challenges.

"As a result, you spend your day thinking about everything that has gone right and can go right. You chase your dreams, and you have a great day, content in where you are and hungry for new achievements that are meaningful to you. You feed yourself nourishing thoughts and good food. You take care of yourself and the ones that you love. You sit in the new rooms that you are building, so to speak.

"Every accomplishment becomes a new room in your virtual castle. You have left and locked the door of your room of despair. You are building anew, and after every achievement, you are revved up to keep accomplishing. You think of your gains and are grateful for them all.

"If you can, lend a hand to others who are struggling in the same pit of depression that you still battle with, because now you can show them hope. You help them out, you play the part of one or more rungs on their ladder. You know that there is hope for them to get out and you do your best to help.

"You know that once they get out, things can get better for them; they can have a better life. This is how you want the rest of your life to go: new challenges, new goals, new achievements, helping yourself and others. Life can be different than it is right now. You can make it different. You have to make the choices though. It is all up to you. You have the power."

Joseph responded, "All right, I will try, but I am real tired. I don't know if I can say that I have had enough. I have to think about it. Maybe I will come up with my own word. I do not particularly like yours and I think it is a little strange."

"No problem. I am not attached to the word Zehhu. I am attached to the concept of Zehhu and its power to stop the descent of depression. So no worries, I would be thrilled if you get your own word, whatever it might be, to help you stop the descent into the pit. Find a way to commit to saying you have had enough and stop."

SUMMARY OF ZEHHU

The summary of Zehhu can be stated in one word: Enough! This seems simple enough to understand, yet not too easy to implement, especially when our minds are saturated with memories of failure and humiliation and our bodies are inundated with feelings of anxiety, fear, anger, and disappointment, the general negative emotions which people who live in depression are pretty familiar with. At the minimum, the first choice you must make is the willingness and commitment to stop the descent. Make the choice that you have had enough and that you want to change course.

Are you ready to refuse the spiral down into deeper depression? If at the least you can muster up the strength to stop the descent, this is the first step I am suggesting you take for yourself. Learn to say you have had enough. Learn to say Stop. Learn to say Zehhu. Be willing to tell yourself to stop, that you have had enough of depression and are going to stop right where you are now and not fall deeper into the pit.

Then start working on climbing out of that hole of depression, rung by rung, until you are back on top of the earth with the rest of the world. It is not your time to live under the ground now. It is time to live above ground and create the best life you can. This is a choice that you must make. Nobody will ever give you more power than you can give to yourself. With as much emotion and passion that you inject in describing the events, circumstances, and people which are at the root of your depression, choose Zehhu with that same passion and stop the slide.

If you have to, scream "Zehhu," or whatever word in whatever language you desire. You have had enough. If you are in public and others will think that you have gone mad, then just shout it to yourself internally, "Zehhu." You are not saying what you will do, but you are saying that you are done with living in the pit of depression. You are willing to stop. You have had enough. Imagine yourself stopping the slide into the quicksand. Just stop doing everything that you do when you are in your depression.

Stop the moping, sulking, repeating the stories, thinking of the stories, people, and events that rile you up. I am not saying to go dance in the streets. I am saying that you make the choice to stop all your depression activities. For instance, if you always consume Ben & Jerry's vanilla Heath bar crunch when you are depressed, then stop. If you always smoke a pack when depressed, stop. If you always get into arguments with yourself or others about a specific topic, stop. Whatever the habits that revolve around your depression, that help to keep the fire-breathing dragon of depression alive that kills your own life, stop feeding it!

Try it for a day, representing the new day after Zehhu. See if you can live more on that day than your typical day of depression. Perhaps your day of depression was unique and so will your new day be unique. Change it up, flip the script, try it out for one day, and if it feels good, keep going. If not, adjust and keep making your days better. This is the first step to getting out of the prison of depression. Say enough in whatever language speaks to you.

THE VINEYARD

"Hello, Joseph, how are things going?"

"Not so great, I don't know. Everything is a mess."

"Sorry to hear that. Did you say Zehhu?"

"I wish I could say yes, but no, I did not."

"I understand. Are you up to speaking today?"

"Yes, I can talk a bit. One thing I wanted to ask you was, let's say I could say Zehhu, so what? What do I do after stopping the slide? What do I do then?"

"Good question. After I had that Zehhu nightmare, even though I stopped the slide and was not having suicidal ideation, I really had no clue how to better cope with depression.

"Let me tell you about a trip that I took to a vineyard. You would not think there is much of a connection between getting out of depression and a vineyard, but I tell you that there can be.

"Of course, every person is different, so perhaps the lessons from a vineyard might be more meaningful to me and you could be inspired by something other than a vineyard. For me, it was the vineyard, and the lessons from the vineyard are the keys. If you can draw out similar lessons from something else, go for it."

"This I have to hear. Zehhu was already strange enough. What could a vineyard have to do with fighting depression, yours or mine?"

"Since that trip, I have been referring to my own struggle of coping with depression as 'planting a vineyard,' and here is why: I believe that a vineyard can teach us about rebuilding our lives and crossing the bridge from depression to life. I believe that a vineyard, and probably many other aspects of nature, can help in the treatment of depression. I refer to the vineyard as my main metaphor because it was there, at a vineyard, that I first had the idea of how to cross the bridge from depression to life. I have experienced for myself that the beauty of nature, thinking about the actions of growing a vineyard, can be just as powerful in fighting depression as Prozac, Zoloft, Risperdal, and Effexor."

"I have suffered from the side effects of many different antidepressant medications. I would be thrilled to just look at a vineyard and be healed instead of popping those pills."

"Well, it is not just looking at a grapevine or a bunch of grapes. There is more. Let me tell you if you have a little time."

"You know me at this point, I have no appointments and I will not be hearing from my children—"

"Joseph, please stop ruminating on everything that is wrong in your life. I know that pain, and it is overwhelming. It is deep, the type of pain that any estranged parent can relate to as well as other people who have experienced traumatic loss. But there are other people out there who are depressed for different reasons. We are not the only people on the planet who are depressed.

So, whatever the reason for someone to fall into the state of depression, once a person is there, it is painful and difficult to explain to someone else who has never felt that type of anguish and hopelessness.

I was once explaining the deep hole in my heart to a doctor and he said, "Ah, what is the big deal, Benjamin, you just move on with your life, just move forward. That is all you have to do." I asked if he has kids. He said no. I asked about a dog. He said, yes, he loves dogs. I asked if he had ever lost a dog. When he answered, he already had tears in his eyes about a dog that he had for over ten years and for whom he had deep emotional attachments.

I said, "You see, Doc? You are getting sentimental about your dog, and I should not about my children? I respect your pain even though I have not experienced it because I have never had a dog. At least you can get a sense of my pain when I tell you about the pain of estrangement from my own children."

He nodded sheepishly; he could now understand. "So I get it, your pain is not going away fast, but if you want to move beyond living in that pain, you have to stop sitting there and find a way to move forward."

In truth, the doctor was right, because everything that we are speaking about is the strategy of how to move forward, but I was missing the map. How do you get from one place to another? How do you cross the bridge from where you are to where you want to be? You need directions and/ or a map to get from your home to a target location. Without a map, saying move forward from the "state of depression" to a "state of living" is like saying you should travel from your home to another location with no map or directions.

"Even for a native New Yorker like you," I said to Joseph as I related my story, "if I asked you to meet me in Port Washington, New York, without directions, a map, or GPS, would you know how to get there?"

"Nope."

"Now that is going from a place in the state of New York to another location in the state of New York. Imagine attempting to go from the state of depression to the state of living, which is like a different planet."

"I cannot imagine what it would feel like to be out of depression. It does seem like a mirage, a different world."

"I know that there are different opinions on the matter, but I have found it to be more advantageous to think of depression as a state of being, similar to a geographical location. Somehow, you, I, anyone else who struggles with depression, arrived there through either genetics and/or a set of events or circumstances, some beyond our control.

"The question now," I told him, "is once we became 'citizens' of that state, can we ever get out? I believe that the answer is yes. We can cross the bridge that leads from the state of depression to the state of living again, for we both know that depression is not 'living.'"

"Fine, so how is the vineyard a map out of the state of depression?"

"One day, I decided to take a trip out of the City to Wölffer Estate, a vineyard that I had seen listed as one of the best in Long Island. I had spent many years languishing and isolated in my apartment, just like you have done for the last decade. Leaving my safe cocoon of depression was a challenge on a few levels, especially momentum. I had no momentum at all. A body at rest stays at rest, they say, and it sure was true for me.

"Nevertheless, it had been a long time since I had been out of the City and I wanted to see the touted vineyards of Long Island. Apparently, over the last few decades, some great vineyards have been growing in our own backyard here in New York State, as hard as that was for me to believe, so I rented a car and made a two- or three-hour trip out to Wölffer Estate on the east end of Long Island to see the phenomenon.

"The estate itself was beautiful and the peaceful surroundings of the ordered rows of vines basking in the setting sun were so calming, not to mention the wine. A vineyard is first of all, an awesome sight to behold, especially at sunset. Not much can compare with acres upon acres of vines on trestles with sparkling grapes cascading and glistening in the sun. There is great order in the vineyard as there is in most other natural wonders of the world, whether it is sunrise or the seasons of the year.

"I was mesmerized by rows upon rows of vines, stretching as far as I could see. I started to think about the time and energy that had gone into creating such a masterpiece. Yes, I had seen farms, corn, olive trees, strawberry fields, but for some reason, seeing the vineyard had a more profound effect. My guess is because I know that the vineyard's purpose is as a bottle of wine.

"Wine is so elegant and classy, since the most ancient of times; and such a precious commodity literally growing on the vines of the trestles was just inspiring.

"I thought that if wine can be created from the dirt, why could I not try to create a better life out of my 'dirt,' the ruins of my life that I had been wallowing in for close to a decade?

"One unique aspect of the vineyard is the time it takes to attain the 'perfect' development, to become wine that is savored and treasured by us, the drinkers, whether or not we are connoisseurs. As opposed to a field of wheat that might take only months to grow, harvest, grind, and bake into a finished bread, a vineyard can literally take years until the desired wine is achieved. It takes time. It takes order. It takes consistency of growth, nourishment, a good environment, care, attention, and commitment to tend the vineyard.

"It was there, at the Wölffer vineyard, that I thought about order, consistency, time for growth, aspiring toward the goal of creating wine out of my life for myself and others to enjoy. It was there at the vineyard where I began to think that perhaps I could find a way to work my own field so to speak, meaning myself, and produce more than weeds, but fine wine, the best version of myself that I could create."

"Sounds a bit too dramatic and farfetched for my taste," Joseph commented. "I still do not see how looking at a vineyard or thinking about the vineyard will do anything for me. I am still stuck with my problems, stuck in this room, stuck on meds, and stuck with this depression and estrangement which has sucked the life out of me. How is looking at a vineyard going to help me with that?"

"I am not judging. I am just saying that we can get some ideas of how to rebuild our lives from what it takes to create a vineyard.

"Nature can be a great teacher," I continued. "During those hours at Wölffer Estate, I felt like it was clear to me that in order to create 'wine' in my life, I needed both time and consistency of effort, and focus toward an end in mind, similar to one of Stephen Covey's seven effective habits: begin with the end in mind.[6] There is no doubt that when those vineyards were planted, the owners began with the end in mind. Their vision was to create fine wine, which would enjoy the praise and devotion of both your average wine lover and true wine connoisseurs.

"When a person has a clear vision in mind, a goal that inspires them, just about anyone can become energetic, aggressive, and dedicated. They do not want to stop till they reach the finish line. For some people, their

6   https://www.stephencovey.com/7habits/7habits-habit2.php

inspiration is art; for others it is music, money, or love. We have to zero in on the fine wine in our life that we want to create, that will inspire us to take action and move beyond our pain. For many years, my field had been overgrown with weeds and thorns. No one was really tending to the land, specifically me. Can you relate to that?"

"Yes, of course."

"At one time, you and me, our lives resembled a successful vineyard. Luscious grapes and fine wine were being produced, there was some acclaim, the vineyard had its beauty, and we were moving along from one year to the next, taking care of the vineyard as we knew best with the awareness we had at the time. There was a time in our lives when we were like the vineyard; we were productive. We were not sitting and mourning in depression; we were working, producing, and doing the best we could at the time. You were also successful, were you not?"

"Yes," Joseph replied. "I studied many years, got my master's degree, and was teaching for almost twenty years when the unthinkable happened. I still do not get, though, how seeing the vineyard got you even remotely interested to get back on your feet. What did you see or imagine that made the difference?"

"I imagined myself as the owner of the vineyard. I imagined that I had a productive field, award-winning wines spread over acres, with my home on the same land and my family inside. I imagined that one day, a tornado ripped through my vineyard, destroying everything that I loved in its path: my children, home, and life. Just like you and anyone else in the world that loses so much, what was my life worth if I no longer had what was most important to me? Everything was uprooted, tossed around like rag dolls, and devastated to the point of not being recognizable. I imagined myself sitting in the middle of this once beautiful field mourning over the destruction of what I had built over a period of decades that took less than a minute to destroy.

"I imagined myself mourning over the irreplaceable losses of family, business, and identity, everything that the vineyard represented for many years. I just sat and could not move. I would sit in the middle of the scorched earth where nothing grew. There were no vines; no kids playing, laughing, or even fighting. There was no longer a home or business and there was no rhyme or reason to life.

"I was not only catatonic, but I saw no point in living. Have you gotten to that point?"

"Of course, almost every night I hope that when I close my eyes, I will wake up to a world where everything that happened was just a nightmare, and when I open my eyes, I realize that I just had a bad nightmare, and I am so relieved that it was just a dream. I will go back to work as usual and see my kids as usual, nothing changed other than waking up out of that nightmare. But then I realize that my reality is my nightmare. When I think that the nightmare is not going to end, that is when I want to end it. I do not want to open my eyes again to this mental torment."

"That is how I first imagined the owner of the vineyard thinking," I told Joseph. "I could see him grappling with the resignation of what would be the point of trying to do that again? The vineyard owner had already worked hard, spent too much time building, and it was all for naught. Why bother again?"

"Yes, that has been me. Why bother again? Why try? I just want to be at peace and close my eyes and not think about everything that I keep thinking about, which just forces me into a deeper level of depression, one that I can never escape."

"For many years, and I think you can relate," I said, "I just was not able to plant anymore, or till the soil, water it, fertilize it, put up the trestles, take care of the vineyard, harvest the grapes, press them, and create awesome wines. It can be destroyed again. Another tornado could come and ravage every last cluster of grapes left on the vine like a tsunami that rushes ashore and removes life in an instant. That is the truth. Life is so fragile. Without a breath, in less than a couple of minutes, we cannot live. Life is so fragile and we all know the truth. At some point in the future, when we go back to the earth, it is as if we did not exist previously. Here today, gone tomorrow. The world keeps turning. Nature continues whether we exist or not.

"I imagined that the morning after the tornado struck, the vineyard owner, who had been so reliant on good weather and always looked at weather as the main component of the vineyard's success, was in shock that the weather to which he entrusted his life became a storm that took away everything that was important to him. This is the life of a person who experiences great loss. Some people have to wait until the end of their life to lose what is most important to them. The vineyard owner did not have to wait. You did not have to wait. Like any person I have ever met who struggles with depression, it feels like the end has already come, and that can happen anytime, even in a person's prime. I then started to wonder what the vineyard owner would do now. If you were the owner of this spectacular vineyard that took you most of your life to create, and it was totally destroyed, what would you do? How long would you sit in your empty field?"

"When you put it that way, I think I would try to find a way to recreate what I once had. I know it would be different, but what is the point of just sitting there?"

"Exactly, there is no point in just sitting in the middle of the field doing nothing. But it took me too long to realize that. For many years, I grieved over my own losses but fortunately, after I went to the vineyard, I started to think about the situation from a different angle. I realized that I still own my land. I am still conscious, and I still have the means to till the soil and plant a vineyard. I am sure we are not the only ones who have faced crushing losses in life. Tornadoes happen. They are freaks of nature, aberrations of the norm, but they do occur. How do we recover? Clearly, some people rebuild, some do not. I was definitely in the latter group for too long. When I went to the Wölffer vineyard, I thought about how many years I had sat in my own land and just accepted the devastation, letting it lie fallow, letting the land dry up and crack, producing no wine. The destruction caused by the tornado was yes, a tragedy, but the even greater tragedy had been me sitting in it for so long. The bigger tragedy has been not utilizing my existing land and capabilities to produce a new successful vineyard and wine that makes me and others happy."

"Yes, that is a tragedy," Joseph agreed. "This ongoing depression is literally killing me."

"I thought about the vineyard and how its existence changes the landscape. I felt that I could plant again if I worked at it. If I got off the ground, dusted myself off, and started digging with my tools. I believed that I could start to transform my property. Can you see yourself picking yourself up, getting off of the ground, working your field, and recreating your vineyard?"

Joseph sighed. "I don't know. It has been a long time. I really don't know if I even have the physical strength, because I have been so wiped out. I feel exhausted. How did you apply the vineyard practically? What did you do or think different?"

"When I came back to the City, I thought about how I could best begin to implement these ideas. I imagined myself as the owner of the vineyard who wants to rebuild. I went out to my property (myself) that had essentially been a wasteland for over a decade. I looked at it. I know it will be a challenge, but if I do not take the plunge now, then when will I have a chance? I apologized to my field for not taking care of it, for not working the land that I had received as a pure gift.

"I resolved to work the land again, little by little, to be patient with my progress and to keep the vision of producing wine in my mind. I resolved to identify goals that are good for me and good for all who will 'drink my wine and taste my herb.'[7] The vineyard teaches us to establish order, to become more disciplined and patient. The vineyard teaches us

---

7   An allusion to "Businessmen they drink my wine, come and taste my herb" from the Jimi Hendrix version of "All Along the Watchtower," which was originally

to toil in the field with the end in mind, with the vision of producing a life that is sweet to ourselves and pleasant to others.

"I literally stumbled across a treatment for depression in the woods. How many medications did I try which did not offer me any perspective, just the feeling of being tranquilized? This is what the vineyard, the simple beauty and order of the vineyard, did for me. It helped to change my thoughts, and once I changed my thoughts to something other than my losses, I started to focus on rebuilding, which instantly made me feel better in my mind than anything else I had tried in the previous ten years.

"I also remembered that in the ancient story of Noah and the flood, the first thing Noah did when he emerged from his ark was to plant a vineyard. 'And Noah began to be a master of the ground, and he planted a vineyard.'[8] When one of the most ancient documents known to the world describes how civilization was rebuilt after the complete destruction of all life by the biblical flood, planting a vineyard was the first step.

"I wondered, why plant a vineyard? Why not plant vegetables or berries that will grow faster? A grapevine can take up to three years to produce viable grapes, a timeline which is based on several environmental factors as well as how you care for the plant. Sunlight and well-drained soil are critical for grape production, as is proper pruning.

---

written by Bob Dylan. It has been voted the 48th greatest hit of all time by *Rolling Stone* magazine. http://en.wikipedia.org/wiki/All_Along_the_Watchtower

8   Genesis Chapter 9 Verse 20.

"If you have neglected an older grapevine, it could stop producing until it gets some attention from you. The bottom line, though, is that most grapevines give you fruit in their third season.[9] Therefore, the plain meaning of that verse cannot be that this grapevine was planted for food. If that were the case, Noah and his family would have starved by the time the grapes were ripe and ready for eating, not to mention the aging necessary to become wine, which can take another one to ten years.

"Clearly, the writer is not teaching us that Noah planted the vineyard for food. To feed his family, Noah might have chosen one of the fastest growing vegetables like radishes, onions, lettuce, baby carrots, kale, and other leafy greens.[10] I think the message of the vineyard is not to tell us what Noah planted for food, but rather the mindset that he needed in order to recover from the greatest worldwide devastation ever documented in history."

"That is interesting; I am familiar with the story and never gave it much thought. Perhaps there is something to be learned from planting a vineyard after a 'flood' of depression that destroys our own world."

"Exactly. I believe there are lessons to be learned from the first story in history that details the actions taken by a person after unparalleled devastation and loss. There are those of us who drown in a sea of despair when our lives are flooded with unexpected events, loss, family estrangement, and/or divorce.

"On one hand, they are unexpected because none of us imagines growing up in a life that is tinged by suffering. On the other hand, we all know that everyone faces their own challenges and some people are knocked down so hard that they never believe they can recover. Our stories and those of any other person who is suffering from depression are different, but they have brought us to a similar place.

---

9   http://homeguides.sfgate.com/long-grape-vines-produce-grapes-56962.html
10   http://www.growthis.com/12-fastest-growing-vegetables/

"Our worlds were devastated by a flood that erased our ability to enjoy life and affected our will to live. In each instance, the flood that haunts us is individual, as it can be precipitated by physical violence, crime, accidents, divorce, loss of relationships, emotional abuse, war, genocide, racism, and/or hate. Some people are more capable of swimming and surviving in an ocean of tears, while others are more susceptible to drowning. But there is a light at the end of the tunnel, with or without medications. Are you open to see what lessons we can glean from the concept of 'planting a vineyard' to recover from the flood of depression?"

"Sure," Joseph said. "I hate being depressed even though I am so used to it. People probably think that I prefer being depressed to being happy."

"I hope that you will feel motivated and able to make changes which are practically free of charge. They have no side effects, other than positive ones, a fitter mind and body that can help us in the battle against depression."

"Okay, so let me think about all that you have said today. I know I can be negative as if I am bleeding all over you. That is the main reason I do not speak to anyone about my thoughts. But with you I can safely tell you all my negative thinking and you do not run away, so I do appreciate your taking the time to reach out to me."

"I am not running away. I am here for you. I am in the same place as you, just moving on a new path that might be beneficial for you as well. I make no judgments. Next time we speak, I will tell you the lessons of the vineyard to cross the bridge from the state of depression to the state of living once again."

Lessons of the Vineyard

CHOOSE TO PLANT YOUR VINEYARD

The premise of these steps is just as a real vineyard requires specific steps to ensure the eventual success of the vineyard, so too does coping with depression. The underlying theory is that we are our own field. As long as we exist, we have the potential to bear fruit just as a field can be cultivated to produce. However, before the edge of the blade of a plow touches the ground that you select to grow your vineyard, the very first action is in our mind. You have to make the choice that you want to grow a vineyard.

The owner of a vineyard makes the decision to plant a vineyard and produce wine; so too you must make the decision to create your own wine, a life that is sweet, pleasant to you and others, without the bitterness of depression. Make the decision now to plant your vineyard. Make the choice now that you want to overcome the depression you are in and be willing to take the necessary actions to make that happen. You have to know your reasons. They might include:

- ✓ A happier life, as it is next to impossible to be happy when you are depressed.
- ✓ A closer and more connected family, since it is devastating for your relatives and loved ones to endure your depression.
- ✓ A healthier life, since it has been demonstrated that depression has catastrophic effects on our immune system, on our ability to sleep and eat well, and on our cortisol levels, which rise and in turn cause us to get fatter, which in turn leads to even deeper depression.

Depression can lead to suicidal ideation and ultimately suicide itself as it is a known fact that depression is the greatest risk factor for suicide.

More than 90% of people who commit or attempt suicide have clinical depression or another diagnosable mental disorder.[11] Know your reasons and get motivated. The motive may be your own health and happiness, or that of your future or present wife, husband, significant other, children, grandchildren, friends, and neighbors. I suggest we look at ourselves as both the field and the owner of the field simultaneously, so even before the first seed is planted, the farmer, owner, viticulturist[12] must make the decision to plant the vineyard.

Therefore, the first step to getting out of depression is to make the decision to start a vineyard and create wine out of your life.

Action Plan

Make the decision to plant a vineyard and create wine out of your life.

---

11 http://www.webmd.com/depression/guide/depression-recognizing-signs-of-suicide
12 The owner of a vineyard is called a viticulturist.

LESSONS OF THE VINEYARD

SELECT A SUNLIGHT DRENCHED LOCATION TO PLANT YOUR VINEYARD

Now that you have made the choice to start your vineyard, the next step is to select the site for your vines.

"This is a fundamental aspect of starting a vineyard, because if you don't know how to grow grapes and keep the vines healthy, you may not achieve success. Grapes have certain needs for best results, including specific climate, temperature, and moisture, along with soil and planting conditions.

Study the climate of the area where you plan to start a vineyard to be sure that grapes will successfully grow there. As a rule, grapes thrive in areas with warm summers, short, mild winters, and few chances for frost. Grapevines also do best with plenty of well-drained moisture and direct sunlight. Keep in mind that grape plants do well on slopes because it helps to properly drain the soil. They also do best with full sun and little or no shade."[13]

To have a successful vineyard, you need the right soil, weather, and moisture, and ample sunlight. Since grapes thrive in areas with warm summers and few chances for frost, we have the best chance of dealing with depression when we can keep the "climate" of our mood, our own

---

13 http://www.wikihow.com/Start-a-Vineyard

personal weather that we control, tilted more to direct sunlight than to frigid cold.

The vineyard needs as much sun as possible, so a person with depression needs to fill her/his mind with sunlight, which means positive thoughts, hopeful thoughts, affirmations, a good attitude, and ultimately a "bright" mind. You can call it corny but what benefit do you have from brooding, sulking, and living in the darkness of depression? Any person in depression is most likely in their own theater much of the time, playing free movies of the painful past.

You know all the dialogue. You are the screenwriter, the director, the producer, and you have the lead role. You will get the Oscar for your performances since you are the academy and the audience all combined. However, is this the movie you want to be playing and repeating and viewing and judging for the rest of your life?

Only you can answer that question. Only you have the power to change the channel, to put on a different movie, to develop a new screenplay of the present and/or the future, because you have no other power than the present and the future. Planting a vineyard with direct sunlight means that you have made the choice to create wine out of your life and now you are selecting the best part of your field, your mind, to begin the process.

A good mind, good thoughts, good ideas fueled by hope and optimism will trump thoughts of defeat and failure any day. When was the last time you were itching to go to a park in nasty, rainy, or stormy weather? Do you expect that people around you, including yourself, want to visit your field, your home, you, when you exude dark, stormy clouds of depression? Perhaps in the beginning, they will try to help you out of the storm, but eventually they will have to save themselves first and let go of you.

You cannot complain that no one is there for you when you are a constant storm of bad personal weather. You should strive to have a better temperament, a more pleasant and inviting personal weather. Your family and friends for sure want to experience you as the picture of sunny weather with clear blue skies. One of the best ways for you to change your personal weather is tied to what you are thinking. Direct sunlight, using the metaphor of the vineyard, means your thoughts. The sentences in your mind are affecting your personal weather.

Let me take a guess of what you might be thinking about a good part of the day in the last week, month, year, and possibly a good part of your life, or since you went into full-blown depression:

- I suck
- I am a failure
- I was no good so my kids do not call me
- I was a bad father/mother so my kids hate me
- I wish I were never born
- I hate my life
- I hate the world
- I hate everyone around me
- I want to die
- I do not want to wake up
- They (everyone you are at war with within your mind) are evil
- They are bad
- I have no friends
- I am always alone
- I am lonely
- I am sad
- I am depressed
- I am worthless
- I am useless
- I am nothing
- I wasted my life
- I regret everything
- I have no future
- I will live in this perpetual shock of estrangement from others and myself forever till I am gone

- I want to scream and cry at the same time
- Why does no one care or listen?
- Why do these medications suck so much?
- How can I get rid of myself as fast as possible so that I do not have to live with this mental pain? I cannot take it!

"How does that sound?" I asked Joseph when I spoke to him again. "Does it ring a bell? Have you ever thought like that? Do you want to spend time with someone whose mind is full of that? Do you think anyone else wants to spend time with a person who has those thoughts day and night?"

"I feel ashamed," Joseph replied. "Those are my thoughts, almost to a tee, how do you know?"

"Those are the same thoughts that were raining in my mind for so many years. I am not saying that I am totally out of the woods, because I can slip back into that type of mental climate like anyone else, but now I am aware of the thoughts that bring me down. The trick now is to start thinking differently. That is the only way I know to bring that direct sunlight into your field. Medication might help you minimize the obsessive thinking, but for me medications did not help to change the type of thoughts I was having, just the way I was feeling, which was generally more tranquilized. So better thoughts are critical to changing your personal climate, whether or not you are using medications."

"What kind of thoughts do you suggest?" Joseph asked. "Can they really help me? Is there such a thing as just thinking different thoughts and changing my personal weather as you call it? Can that help me get out of depression? Will that get my daughters back? I am willing to do anything…"

"Don't cry, Joseph, because that has no chance of getting your daughters back. Try some of the following thoughts. You will have to keep thinking them a lot, because you have thought the opposite for so long. You have to spend a lot of time healing your mind from within by going to the opposite extreme. I know it will feel strange at first, but give it a shot. You have nothing to lose and everything to gain."

- I love and approve of myself[14]
- I am good
- I am successful
- I did the best that I could at the time and I do not know the thoughts of my kids, but I know that they want the best for me too
- I was the best parent that I could be and I know that my kids do love me
- I am grateful that I am here and have an opportunity to build a new life
- I am excited about creating a new present and bright future
- I appreciate the world around me
- I appreciate the people around me and can see the good within them
- I am grateful to be alive and create fine wine out of my life
- I am grateful to get a good night's sleep and wake up early in the morning to seize another day of potential
- I cannot get into the minds of "so and so'" I appreciate that I am aware and live in my mind and not theirs
- I cannot control anyone else's thoughts but I can control mine and that is where my power is, in my mind, my field, my life
- I appreciate that I can focus on myself and build a better future

"If you can get into the habit of being a good weatherman for your own thoughts, you might start to see results in your own feelings

---

14 "I love and approve of myself" is one of the best affirmations out there because it treats the self-loathing and rejection that a depressed person has of themselves. I first read this affirmation from Louise Hay in her book *You Can Heal Your Life*. See the book for more excellent affirmations.

throughout the day, in being more optimistic, and in becoming more productive. Of course there is going to be a better chance that when your field is blooming, more people, friends, relatives, and maybe even your daughters are going to want to visit."

In addition to the idea of the sun as being brighter thoughts, we can also see the idea of the sun and sunlight to mean the physical sunlight, which includes getting outside in the sun when possible and the many physical smiles which you can start to practice in order to manage depression. The sun is a universal symbol of a smiling happy face. It is not difficult to understand why the sun easily represents happiness and smiling. When the sun comes out, people are naturally happier than when the sun is hidden on a cloudy day, especially on a cold day. The warmth of the sun heals, gives light, enables vegetation to grow, gives us vitamin D, generates life, and sustains life. The sun does all of this without bias and without cost.

No matter who you are, young or old, man or woman, good or bad, sinner or saint, any race, gender, creed, sexual orientation on the planet, the sun will grow your vegetables and the sun will nourish you without discrimination. Without the sun, nothing in the world can survive.

The sun provides light, heat, and photosynthesis, the process of how plants use sunlight to make food from carbon dioxide and water; in fact, 99.9 percent of the natural productivity on Earth is done by photosynthesis, which requires the sun.

Without the sun, plants would no longer be able to inhale carbon dioxide and exhale the life-sustaining oxygen that we breathe.

The sun provides gravity, which keeps the earth in orbit.[15]

Without your own internal sunshine, can you survive? When our internal sun disappears and we are depressed, we experience the absence of light, confusion, coldness of existence. We experience leaving our

---

15 http://www.huffingtonpost.com/2013/04/03/what-if-the-sun-disappeared-earth-video_n_2999693.html

orbit, we lose control, center of gravity, and become unstable and 'far out there, over the edge.' Just as the sun is the generator and sustainer of life, celebrates life and happiness, gives and nourishes life, so too our internal sunlight is what keeps us going and growing.

Without the sun and our internal sun, life on the planet stops and our life feels as if it has ceased. Our internal sun gives us energy and enables us to keep breathing and keep going despite the challenges that we all face.

Without the sun, nothing living in the world would survive. Without it we cannot see or be warm; we are lost. It is just like Albert Einstein said: There is no actual darkness. It is just the term we use for the absence of light. There is no cold, for it is only the absence of heat.

"Perhaps we can extrapolate and say that a feature of depression is the absence of our own internal sun; the light, warmth, energy, and internal oxygen that keeps a person alive, optimistic, and hopeful no matter what.

The sun keeps everything alive and similarly we must maintain our internal sun.

Selecting the right site for a vineyard teaches us an important lesson. Find your internal sun. A person battling depression must do what is necessary to maximize both the external and internal sunlight in her/his life. Sunlight is free and similarly, the first steps to overcoming depression cost nothing, requires little effort other than the thoughts required to maintain internal sunlight, and has well-known scientifically demonstrated benefits.

In addition to your internal sun, what physical action is free, costs nothing, takes no effort and can bring sun into your life besides the role of positive thinking to generate your own internal sunlight? The first physical step is to start smiling. How can a depressed person even attempt to have a more upbeat disposition? By definition, if you are depressed, it should be impossible to smile and even appear happy. You always appear brooding and angry.

Do you only smile when you are happy, or can smiling actually influence your mood to feel happy? In 1989, a psychologist named Robert Zajonc published one of the most significant studies on the emotional effect of producing a smile. His subjects repeated vowel sounds that forced their faces into various expressions. To mimic some of the characteristics of a smile, they made the long "e" sound, which stretches the corners of the mouth outward. Subjects reported feeling good after making the long "e" sound, and feeling bad after the long "u." The evidence points toward smiling as a cause of happy feelings. Subjects were asked questions that highlighted their emotional state before and after smiling, and they overwhelmingly scored happier after smiling.

Even proponents of the theory do not suggest that smiling can make unhappiness go away. The theory basically states that in a state of emotional neutrality, putting a smile on your face can tip you in the direction of a positive feeling.[16] If that is not enough evidence for you to start smiling right now, here are 10 more:

The Top 10 Reasons to Smile[17]

1. Smiling Makes Us Attractive - We are drawn to people who smile. There is an attraction factor. We want to know a smiling person and figure out what is so good. Frowns, scowls, and grimaces all push people away—but a smile draws them in.

2. Smiling Changes Our Mood - Next time you are feeling down, try putting on a smile. There's a good chance your mood will change for the better. Smiling can trick the body into helping you change your mood.

3. Smiling Is Contagious - When someone is smiling they lighten up the room, change the mood of others, and make things

16 http://science.howstuffworks.com/life/smiling-happy3.htm
17 By Mark Stibich, Ph.D. Updated May 16, 2014.

happier. A smiling person brings happiness with them. Smile more and you will draw people to you.

4. Smiling Relieves Stress - Stress can really show up in our faces. Smiling helps to prevent us from looking tired, worn down, and overwhelmed. When you are stressed, take the time to put on a smile. The stress should be reduced and you will be better able to take action.

5. Smiling Boosts Your Immune System - Smiling helps the immune system work better. When you smile, immune function improves because you are more relaxed. Prevent the flu and colds by smiling.

6. Smiling Lowers Your Blood Pressure - When you smile, there is a measurable reduction in your blood pressure.

7. Smiling Releases Endorphins, Natural Pain Killers, and Serotonin - Studies have shown that smiling releases endorphins, natural pain killers, and serotonin. Together these three make us feel good. Smiling is a natural drug.

8. Smiling Lifts the Face and Makes You Look Younger - The muscles we use to smile lift the face, making a person appear younger. Don't go for a face lift, just try smiling your way through the day and you will look younger and feel better.

9. Smiling Makes You Seem Successful - Smiling people appear more confident, are more likely to be promoted, and more likely to be approached. Put on a smile at meetings and appointments and people will react to you differently.

10. Smiling Helps You Stay Positive - Try this test: Smile. Now try to think of something negative without losing the smile. It is hard. When we smile our body is sending the rest of us a message that "Life is good!" Stay away from depression, stress, and worry by smiling.[18]"

---

18 By Mark Stibich, Ph.D. Updated May 16, 2014.

A noted British scientist, Professor Jane Plant, says that smiling can be more effective than Prozac to reduce anxiety, stress, and depression.[19] The truth is that there are many articles and references to bolster the position that increasing your ability to smile, both internally with brighter self-healing thoughts and physically, can have a powerful impact on your success in fighting depression.

Just as grapes thrive in a sun-drenched field, so too will you be able to influence your own mood with arguably the simplest virtual and physical actions that you can take to shower your own field with sunlight—think brighter affirming thoughts, get outside when possible and physically smile. If you want to get a simple, practical, and effective head start to beating your depression, start your bright thoughts and smiling strategy now.

You must have something in your life to smile about, and when you do find it, connect the dots and start to smile. Whatever it is that might make you feel grateful or happy, let those good feelings continue to grow so that you can emerge from the pit of depression and start growing your virtual vineyard.

Action Plan

Start to become aware of your predominant thoughts today. When you notice those that are negative, flip them around to be positive. Start to brighten your mind today with positive thoughts and affirmations.

Get outside when weather permits and start smiling today.

---

19 http://www.theguardian.com/society/2008/jul/27/mentalhealth.drugs

LESSONS OF THE VINEYARD

WORKING YOUR FIELD

The third step in growing a vineyard is to prepare the field from the ground up. The most simple, practical, and effective strategy for fighting depression is to build yourself from the ground up, meaning we must start by working on ourselves, publicly without shame, to improve ourselves as well as improving our physical health. What does it mean to work on ourselves?

You do not work on someone else's field. A person in depression has to stop working in another person's field, in another person's mind. It is easy in the depressed state to say and think how everyone else should be doing this or that. Every time we say that, we are working on someone else's field. Their field is their responsibility.

All our power and ownership is in our field. Stop casting the blame of everything that has gone wrong in our lives into another's field. This does not mean other people might not be at fault at times, but for us, we have the most power when we take ownership. Once you take ownership, you have the power to correct and improve. As long as improvement in your life is dependent on what someone else says or does, then you lose your power.

I call this process "shoulder the shoulds," meaning to take all the shoulds we speak of when referring to other people and place those shoulds on your own shoulders. For example:

"He should treat me with respect" becomes "I should treat me with respect." "She should forgive me" becomes "I should forgive me."

"They should stop ignoring me" becomes "I should stop ignoring and neglecting myself." "They should care about me and help me get better" becomes "I should take better care of myself and do what it takes to become better."

This is a very effective method for you to take back your power. You are the one fighting depression. You are the one who must become as powerful as possible. As long as you are waiting for someone else to do or say something that will make you better or make the situation better, then you are at their mercy. You can just keep sitting in your room and waiting, and there is no guarantee that those outside forces you depend on are even thinking about you. Most likely they are dealing with their own lives and problems that they are facing.

They become distracted and busy with their lives and you put yours on hold till they remember or you remind them of how they should be treating you.

Take back your power now and "shoulder the shoulds." The day you decide to do your best to take care of yourself can be one of the most liberating days of your life.

This acceptance and decision to take ownership and work your field will generate immense power, because you have freed yourself from relying on others to do what you can do for yourself. This is a basic and powerful lesson of the vineyard which teaches us to work on our own field and to stay out of the fields of others. Even though the idea is very clear when we think of it in terms of fields and property, many of us make the mistake of constantly living in the minds of others: "What are they thinking?" "Why doesn't he call?" "Why doesn't she care?"

If you have spent any time in the ROD (Room of Depression) or ROE (Room of Estrangement), you know what I am talking about. Both of those theaters have free showings day and night, and you can pull out the popcorn, goobers, chips, and Ben & Jerry's while watching reruns to your heart's content.

The Room of Depression or Room of Estrangement will pull you down. These "theaters" are all in your mind where you can play and replay the scenes of your past and how you have been hurt, maligned, or disenfranchised, weighing you down deeper into depression.

Much of the time in the theater is spent casting blame on others and exonerating ourselves. They should have, could have, if they would have done that then I would not be depressed. When you are sitting all comfy, scarfing down Oreos and watching those reruns, you are in their field and you are neglecting your own field. One of the most basic truths that we learn from the analogy of planting a vineyard is to stay in our own field and work it. You have the right to work your own field and you are the one responsible, nobody else.

Take back your right and responsibility and you will be taking back your power.

You will be able to get out of the ROD theater, close the door, lock it, and start working on improving your own life in every possible aspect. Get into a theater that does not show many reruns but rather future visions, dreams, goals, scenes, and ideas that motivate you and make you feel energized to take action. Get into a theater that promises you a good crop, or good wine, if you take the actions now to work the field and plant the vines.

You can use this analogy endlessly to start new projects, build new theaters, and create more present and future satisfaction in your life and less pain and frustration.

In the same way we work our field in the open, we can work on ourselves in the open. We do not have to be ashamed that our field was lying in ruins, or feel embarrassed that we fell down, lost our career, lost our family. We became estranged from family or friends, and everything or some things went south.

We do not have to be ashamed when we are picking up the pieces. We have two choices after the vineyard is leveled by a storm. We can just sit there and sulk and remain depressed with the devastation around us, or get up and start rebuilding our vineyard, our lives. I know that it is a lot easier to just sit in the ruins of the vineyard. I know because I did just that for over a decade. Sitting is easier, but we all know that too much sitting results in bad health. Doing nothing cannot create much that is productive in life. Doing nothing is not creating a new life.

One can sit and mourn but by now you or someone you know has already experienced that, and anyone who experiences depression knows that it is not fun, or joyous. Sitting depressed and mourning in our field is not the best option. Get up and start working on putting your life back together. Get up and start working your field, doing what you have to do to get the ground ready to be planted. Start thinking about the new vines that you will be planting, and the future wine that will be on your table. Start motivating yourself with scenes of what you can accomplish.

There is no shame in picking up the pieces. *The shame is doing nothing and surrendering your life to depression.* It is okay to say that at some point in our lives we screwed up, and sometimes we screwed up more than just burning the pizza, and we have to acknowledge that and do what we can to fix that which we can fix today. Stop hiding. An aspect of depression is hiding, shame, embarrassment, isolation, staying out of the public view. Work your field in the open. Stop hiding, get out for a walk, let everything be seen, be transparent, admit where you have failed. You are human, we make mistakes.

It is not enough to have the desire to beat depression. It is not enough to start thinking brighter thoughts and to start smiling more. While these are excellent and important strategies, it is important to work hard in our fields to help expedite the lessening of depression. A strong healthy body will have a greater chance of fighting against depression. This is just common sense.

The vineyard teaches us to bear down and break ground, work the earth, meaning we start building our physical strength for several reasons: A stronger and healthier body will by definition have healthier cells and a healthier physical mind, reduce inflammation, and increase endorphins, all contributing to a better mood. A stronger and healthier body will enable you to focus on doing something productive rather than destructive. Instead of destroying your body with junk food and obsessing on the miseries of the past, disappointing present and/or anxiety-laden future, you will be focused on building your best physical foundation for a healthier life.

"Whether planting or replanting, a vineyard is both figuratively and literally developed from the ground up. Having a thorough understanding of your soil and site is crucial to developing the best vineyard possible for that location. This includes soil depth, structure, chemistry, drainage, and erosion potential. Soil/site preparation is very important. The most important operation in replanting is to do a thorough job of removing old grapevine roots. The best way to remove most root pieces is to deep plow the field."[20]

A plow is a tool used in farming for initial cultivation of soil in preparation for sowing seeds or planting by loosening or turning the soil. Plows are traditionally drawn by working animals such as horses or cattle, but in modern times may be drawn by tractors. A plow may be made of wood, iron, or steel. It has been a basic instrument for most recorded history, and represents one of the major advances in agriculture.

"The primary purpose of plowing is to turn over the upper layer of the soil, bringing fresh nutrients to the surface, while burying weeds, the remains of previous crops, and both crop and weed seeds, allowing them to break down. It also provides a seed-free medium for planting an alternate crop."[21]

Just as plowing removes the roots and buries the weeds of previous crops, so too building your mind and body enables you to move on from the past and bury the weeds of your past. Build a new you. Transform yourself from that person who has endured all of the suffering which

---

20 http://www.practicalwinery.com/janFeb07/janfeb07p91.htm
21 http://en.wikipedia.org/wiki/Plough

has been depressing you till this day and become a new person. You will absolutely feel differently than you did in the past when you look in the mirror and can barely recognize yourself. This is a strong message that you have moved on from the past and that you are moving forward to a better life. The best way to get out of depression is to start moving your body and stop sitting and marinating in the memories and thoughts which destroy all happiness in your life. Can exercising your body really help to reduce depression?

Strength of mind is exercise, not rest.
– Alexander Pope, Poet

Exercise would cure a guilty conscience.
– Plato

Regular aerobic exercise will bring remarkable changes to your body, metabolism, heart, and spirit. It has a unique capacity to exhilarate and relax, provide stimulation and calm, counter depression, and dissipate stress.

It is a common experience among endurance athletes and has been verified in clinical trials that have successfully used exercise to treat anxiety disorders and clinical depression. If athletes and patients can derive psychological benefits from exercise, so can you. How can exercise contend with problems as difficult as anxiety and depression? There are several explanations, some chemical, others behavioral. The mental benefits of aerobic exercise have a neurochemical basis.

Exercise reduces levels of the body's stress hormones, such as adrenaline and cortisol. It also stimulates the production of endorphins, the chemicals in the brain that are the body's natural painkillers and mood elevators. Endorphins are responsible for the "runner's high" and for the feelings of relaxation and optimism that accompany many hard workouts. Behavioral factors also contribute to the emotional benefits of exercise. As your waistline shrinks and your strength and stamina increase, your self-image will improve. You will earn a sense of mastery and control, pride, and self-confidence.

Your renewed vigor and energy will help you succeed in many tasks, and the discipline of regular exercise will help you achieve other important lifestyle goals. Exercise and sports also provide opportunities to get away from it all and to either enjoy some solitude or to make friends and build networks. "All men," wrote St. Thomas Aquinas, "need leisure." Exercise is play and recreation. When your body is busy, your mind will be distracted from the worries of daily life and will be free to think creatively.

Almost any type of exercise will help. Many people find that using large muscle groups in a rhythmic, repetitive fashion works best; call it "muscular meditation," and you will begin to understand how it works. Walking and jogging are prime examples. Even a simple twenty-minute stroll can clear the mind and reduce stress. But some people prefer vigorous workouts that burn stress along with calories. That's one reason elliptical is so popular. The same stretching exercises that help relax your muscles after a hard workout help relax your mind as well.

Regular physical activity will lower your blood pressure, improve your cholesterol, and reduce your blood sugar. Exercise cuts the risk of heart attack, stroke, diabetes, colon and breast cancers, osteoporosis and fractures, obesity, depression, and even dementia (memory loss). Exercise slows the aging process, increases energy, and prolongs life.

Except during illness, you should exercise nearly every day. That doesn't necessarily mean hitting the gym or training for a marathon. But it does mean thirty to forty minutes of moderate exercise such as walking or fifteen to twenty minutes of vigorous exercise. More is even better, but the first steps provide the most benefit. Aim to walk at least two miles a day, or do the equivalent amount of another activity. You can do it all at once or in ten- to fifteen-minute chunks if that fits your schedule better. Add a little strength training and stretching two to three times a week and you will have an excellent, balanced program for health and stress reduction. Popular beliefs notwithstanding, exercise is relaxing.[22]

Action Plan

Stay in your field, work on yourself, get out of your isolation, start working out.

I am going to give you the basic guidelines that enabled me to lose seventy-five pounds in ten months and lose sixteen inches off my waist, and helped me transform physically. To my surprise, my mood and attitude began to change as well. It is clear that to begin an exercise program which can reduce depression does not require anything more complicated than getting out of your room and taking a walk for at least thirty minutes. If you live in a cold climate and have access to a gym, treadmill, or elliptical, you can still get started.

What is important is that you start working your field physically. Get moving, today. Sitting at home in isolation, reviewing all the reasons why you are in the perpetual shock of depression, will not solve the issue. I empathize with everything that you are going through; I still live with memories and thoughts that could crush me as they have in the past if I let them get the upper hand. I am sure that we are not alone in

---

22 http://www.health.harvard.edu/

that department. Everybody has to deal with challenges from so many potential sources; financial, relationship, career, health, society; the list is quite long.

However, for some reason people are wired in a way where these challenges can morph into depression, not just sadness, but depression that can have catastrophic consequences. Simple exercises like walking, swimming, biking, elliptical, treadmill, anything that gets you moving for one to two miles, even just thirty minutes a day, can be the foundation of a life-changing regimen.

In the amount of time that you might watch an episode of Judge Judy berating a litigant for trying to pull a fast one on her and failing, you can test the exercise waters as a method to start pulling you out of depression. My initial prescription when it came to exercise was to start walking for thirty minutes a day. Some days I had access to a pool, so I swam, and other days when it was too cold I used the elliptical. There are five major changes that I made to my lifestyle, which is what led to the dramatic changes that I experienced. They are simple to write, yet more challenging to implement because of our ingrained habits and disbelief that we can transform our body and mind no matter our age and shape. These five new habits will change your physical body the way the plow breaks up the earth and prepares it for planting the vineyard.

Make a commitment to acquire one new habit starting today. One thing that I have learned is not to underestimate the power of consistency and gradual improvement. These are the big four exercise habits to physically "work your field":

✓ Walking
✓ Pushups
✓ Squats
✓ Deadlifts

LESSONS OF THE VINEYARD

WORKING YOUR FIELD
WITH WALKING

Walking is the simplest way to start and is an excellent habit to implement. Walking is a natural form of movement that you can begin to take on a consistent basis. Did you know that today, researchers are actually identifying what they call "sitting disease"? There is so little movement by our culture today due to office jobs and being the audience for entertainment, whether from TV or a concert or a sporting event, that it is now a scientific fact that sitting disease is real. I happened to come across a shocking article about the dangers of sitting. It's called 'Don't Just Sit There! It Could Be Harmful Later in Life,'[23] and you have to read it for yourself to believe it. If this article doesn't put the fear of the chair into you, what will?

Starting a walking program should not be too difficult, but I know firsthand how hard it is to begin. I hope that this might persuade you to get out of your room and start walking, swimming, or doing elliptical. If you can only get out of your room for a minute, do it. Move up to twenty or a minimum of thirty to sixty minutes a day to reap the maximum benefits from walking. Of course, walking is not the only way to get moving. If you prefer swimming, elliptical, treadmill, biking, or rowing,

---

23 http://www.usatoday.com/story/news/nation/2014/02/19/
    sitting-disease-disability-older-adults/5583941/

just do it. The main point, though, is to start moving physically to get past your depression and put distance between you and your depression.

You might say that you can never create that distance because the depression is rooted in your mind wherever you go, but I have found that once you do start moving, those painful memories can be less intense, because you are establishing positive and forward momentum. When I started walking, I did not know there were clinical studies that demonstrated the benefits of walking for depression. Here is one to get you motivated.

Benefits of Walking by Tommy Boone

Walking and Depression

Exercise like walking has been shown to relieve the symptoms of depression. Clinical depression is defined as sadness that is greater and more prolonged than is warranted by any objective reason. It is characterized by withdrawal, inactivity, dullness, and feelings of helplessness and loss of control. For many people suffering from clinical depression, regular exercise (three times a week or more appears to work best) has been shown to act as a mood elevator. Doctors, it seems, are convinced by the evidence in favor of using exercise to treat depression. In a survey of 1,750 doctors, 85 percent reported that they prescribed exercise -- including walking -- for treating depression (and 60 percent prescribed exercise to treat anxiety).

The NIMH panel on the effects of exercise on mental health concluded that long-term exercise reduces depression in people who are moderately depressed. In those who are severely depressed, exercise appears to be a useful addition to professional treatment, including psychotherapy, medication (combining exercise with antidepressant medication demands close medical supervision), and electroshock.

In a University of Wisconsin study, exercise even appeared to be as effective as psychotherapy at relieving moderate depression. People with moderate depression were randomly assigned to either psychotherapy or exercise programs.

After a year, over 90 percent of the people who had been assigned to the exercise program were no longer depressed. Half of the patients in the psychotherapy group, however, had come back for more treatment. Why is walking helpful in the treatment -- and perhaps even the prevention -- of depression? Following any exercise program, including walking, gives participants a sense of self-reliance, self-mastery, power, and control because they are getting out and doing something for and by themselves, says Robert S. Brown, M.D., Ph.D., clinical associate professor of behavioral medicine and psychiatry at the University of Virginia in Charlottesville.

Exercise gives people a real opportunity to set and achieve goals and to see and measure personal improvement. One way to enhance this effect and visualize walking accomplishments is to use a daily log or journal. By writing down the speed of each walk and the distance covered, the walker can keep track of personal improvement. Walking may also promote feelings of pleasure, tranquility, and well-being and help relieve the pain of depression by encouraging the production of the body's natural opiates, called endorphins. These chemical cousins of morphine are responsible for the feeling of euphoria called "runner's high."

Exercise can help distract depressed people from their feelings of sadness. Simply going through the motions of confident striding may be enough to build a walker's confidence. Also, since regular aerobic exercise is an important aid in losing weight and toning muscles, exercisers may feel the general sense of well-being that stems from knowing they look better and feel healthier.

Unlike some more strenuous exercises, walking feels good while you're doing it, not just when you stop.[24] In addition, walking has many other benefits. Some are outlined in an article I read called 'Top 10 Benefits of Walking,' by Michael Roizen, MD, and Mehmet Oz, MD.[25] Just a few of the benefits include more energy and an improved immune system.

"The bottom line is to start walking or doing any other continuous exercise that you can do every day to begin your journey out of depression. I have found that the best time is in the morning; this way you can make sure that you have created a productive habit to take care of yourself first.

If you do not make taking care of yourself a priority, who will? The last vote of confidence that I will give you for walking even up to an hour a day comes from Dr. Chauncey Crandall. No matter what age you are, it makes sense to get in the habit of a healthy lifestyle. Walking is not only effective for boosting your mood and helping you to relieve depression, but even for improving your cardiovascular health, which in turn will lift your mood even further, knowing that you are investing your time in a productive activity that is good for you and those that care about you.

Dr. Crandall makes the following statements about the benefits of walking for patients with heart disease and certainly for people without: Besides improving your heart health, you can also lift your mood. The best exercise is walking one hour per day. Get moving on a daily basis. Start exercising five days a week for one hour per day.

Walking is generally the best exercise available because it doesn't place too much stress on the knees, hips, and back. If you like to run, you may want to mix running into your walks, which is how people have been moving ever since civilization began. You can literally walk heart disease

---

24 http://health.howstuffworks.com/wellness/diet-fitness/exercise/benefits-of-walking6.htm

25 https://www.sharecare.com/health/walking/article/walking-benefits

away. I walk for a full hour every day. I know this sounds simple, but walking for sixty minutes each day requires commitment. The benefits you reap will change your life. Walking is an aerobic exercise, which means your heartbeat is raised for a sustained period of time.

You may have heard that thirty minutes a few times per week is sufficient to keep you healthy. I disagree. In fact, the reason those experts limit their recommendations to thirty minutes is because they don't think that people will have the discipline to walk for a full hour every day. I have more faith. Still, an hour per day can seem like a daunting task.

I usually tell my patients to start with twenty minutes each day for two weeks, and then advance to forty minutes each day for another two weeks. After a month of warming up, they are ready to make the commitment to walking a full hour every day.

I believe that once people understand the biology behind walking an hour every day, and appreciate how it can improve their overall health, they will make the commitment.

Don't Forget Your Second Wind — When you wake up in the morning, or whenever you start to walk, your body has a built-in reserve of energy that lasts for about thirty minutes. The key is to continue walking past that thirty-minute mark and tap into the body's collateral circulatory system.

We are all familiar with the body's circulatory system, which consists of the vessels and muscles that control the blood flow throughout the body. The components of this system include the heart, arteries, veins, and capillaries. What you may not know is that your body also has what's called a "collateral circulatory system," a microscopic network of blood vessels that ordinarily remain closed.

However, with sustained physical activity—such as a daily, hour-long walk—these vessels open and become enlarged, forming an alternate network to bring blood to your heart.

When these vessels open, it causes the "second wind" feeling of prolonged aerobic exercise. In addition, this blood flow can detour around blockages and relieve angina (chest pain that comes from heart disease) or even help to prevent a heart attack. But that's not all a one-hour walk does. As you continue beyond the thirty-minute mark, your body pumps up its production of nitric oxide, a gas that is credited with many benefits, such as helping keep arteries clean of plaque, as well as widening the arteries and keeping them supple. Each of these actions helps lower blood pressure, decreasing the risk of both heart attack and stroke.

As you continue to walk, your body goes through many beneficial processes, such as breaking down the fat in your liver and revving up your metabolism, which converts the sugar in your blood into energy more efficiently. Study after study shows that regular walking helps prevent diabetes (or manage your blood sugar better if you already have the disease). For instance, a study published in the January issue of the *British Medical Journal* found that people who walked 10,000 steps a day as a form of exercise had a sharply reduced risk for diabetes. And how long does it take to walk 10,000 steps a day? About one hour.

Research presented at the American College of Cardiology's annual meeting provided definitive evidence that staying fit keeps your heart young. It is well known that muscle mass diminishes with aging. But this study, which looked at people older than sixty-five, found that the heart of those who stayed the most active looked more youthful than even the hearts of people aged twenty-four to thirty-five. In addition, the heart muscles in these study subjects were flexible. That meant that these older exercisers were less likely to develop diastolic heart failure, a condition in which the heart is unable to pump efficiently enough to keep up with the demands of the body. When you exercise, your body produces endorphins, which are hormones that act as natural mood elevators. This is how activity alleviates depression.[26]

---

26 Crandall, Chauncey (2013-10-08). The Simple Heart Cure: The 90-Day Program to Stop and Reverse Heart Disease (Kindle Locations 1853-1856). Humanix Publishing LLC. Kindle Edition.

At this point, even if you were not suffering from depression, it should be a no-brainer to start walking at the minimum, and as we have said and studies show, walking is the most available, easiest to do, and wildly beneficial form of exercise for just about anyone.

If you are more capable and you are a skier, go ski. For the general population, there is no exercise that levels the playing field like walking for everybody who has the ability to walk.

For those that do not, pick some activity that will give you an aerobic benefit, and for those who can, develop a sense of gratitude that you can and make use of the gifts that you have. Certainly if you are battling depression, getting out of your physical apartment or room and moving your body forward is going to set you up for moving forward virtually in your life.

Whatever it is that you are depressed about is not going to change by your walking a few miles a day, but what will change besides the improvement in your overall health is that you will internalize the sensation of moving past your problems, creating distance between yourself and the root of your depression, leaving your room of depression, working your field to overturn the roots of your depression and allow a new field, a new vineyard, to be planted.

I have spoken mostly about walking because walking is accessible to most people no matter what age or physical condition you are in. However, to give you more food for thought, you should be aware that running is also an excellent option to treat depression. Consider the research from Cambridge University, where scientist Ian Sample says that aerobic exercise triggers new cell growth in your brain and helps with memory recall.[27]

"In another article, Traci Pedersen reports that there are new guidelines for using exercise as an antidepressant, including how often

---

27 http://www.theguardian.com/science/2010/jan/18/
    running-brain-memory-cell-growth

to exercise so you feel better. What researchers recommend is to exercise three to five times a week for about an hour."[28]

Running Testimonials

"Running! If there's any activity happier, more exhilarating, more nourishing to the imagination, I can't think of what it might be. In running the mind flees with the body, the mysterious efflorescence of language seems to pulse in the brain, in rhythm with our feet and the swinging of our arms." - Joyce Carole Oates, American author and professor of creative writing at Princeton University

"When I am running my mind empties itself. Everything I think while running is subordinate to the process. The thoughts that impose themselves on me while running are like light gusts of wind – they appear all of a sudden, disappear again and change nothing." - Haruki Murakami, Japanese Author

"When I run, I think about everything: physics, family problems, plans for the weekend. I haven't made any big discoveries on a run, but it does give me time to think through problems. Some solutions are obvious, but they are only obvious when you are relaxed enough to find them." - Wolfgang Ketterle, Nobel Prizewinning Physicist, MIT

"Being a runner, to me, has made being depressed impossible. If ever I'm going through something emotional and just go outside for a run, you can rest assured that I'll come back with clarity and empowerment." - Alanis Morissette, Singer-Songwriter

---

28 http://psychcentral.com/news/2013/05/11/new-guidelines-for-using-exercise-as-an-antidepressant/54728.html

Action Plan

Start walking today for thirty minutes and keep increasing your time till you get to one hour. If you are capable of running, then start running. You will be in good company.

Lessons of the Vineyard

WORKING YOUR FIELD WITH PUSHUPS

The next simplest exercise that you can begin to do to work your field is the classic pushup. All you need is yourself and a floor and you can start to build an impressive physique with this exercise alone. Remember, building your body is parallel to creating a great field that will grow the vineyards to produce fine wine. Ultimately as you get into better shape, you will find it easier to deal with your depression and I believe that you will experience relief from the depression you are in.

The point is to build a strong healthy body that will result in a clear, stable, even-keeled mind. Pushups are nowhere as easy as walking, but you will reap amazing rewards from the simple push up if you are consistent and patient. Over the course of ten months, I went from only being able to crank out one pushup up to my high of fifty-six pushups. The best part, of course, was discovering that as I got into better shape, I felt better.

All the Effexor, Prozac, Zoloft, Neurontin, Risperdal, Paxil, and other antidepressants that I took for many years never gave me the relief from depression that real food and exercise has together with additional strategies that I will be discussing soon.

While walking is great for your cardiovascular system and all of the other benefits that have been listed above, pushups are going to be your go-to exercise for building upper body strength.

"First, no money is needed for doing pushups. I have been doing them in my apartment for over a year. Yes, I open the windows, get some fresh air, and then do sets till I reach 100. I always start with my max for that day which fluctuates; one day it can be fifty-six, my highest, and one day it can be forty. I find that doing pushups every day might be overtraining, so I have found that three days a week works best for me. You can try every day or every other day as well and take a break on the weekend so your muscles can rest a bit. I would not say the results are immediate, not even after a couple of weeks, but I think it is fair to say that with exercise, along with good eating habits, you can see some good results after a couple of months to a year.

"I think the idea of wanting to see great results after decades of inactivity is not reasonable or rational. If you can only do one pushup, do one and then an hour later do another one. Try to do five for the day and keep improving gradually from there. Three days a week, starting with just one pushup will transform your body and mind over the course of months if you are patient and consistent and eat real food daily.

Pushups are a full-body workout and can help to transform your whole body. They have been the main exercise that I have done besides deadlifts and squats and there is no question that I have experienced a total body transformation, which you can as well

"If you think that pushups are easy, think again. Just get down on your floor and try one. If you can do one, try ten and if you can do ten, then try thirty. If you can do thirty consecutive pushups, you are getting into pretty decent shape. Imagine the shape you will be in when you can do fifty or sixty straight.

"Pushups increase your muscle growth, which is important not only for how you look in your suit, but also for your health. The more muscle the better to fend off aging, diabetes, cardiovascular disease and depression. The more muscle, the more testosterone that you have and the less depressed you are likely to be. Pushups are a great way to increase your muscle growth literally one day at a time, or if you want to have an in between rest day, every other day at a time.

"Pushups also help you avoid injuries when you do other types of weight-training exercises. I use pushups to this day to warm up for my shoulder presses. In the past, I had a shoulder injury on my left shoulder and I was very reluctant to ever try an overhead press again. But since I have been doing pushups, my shoulders have gotten stronger and I do my pushups sets before doing shoulder presses.

"The truth is if you just did walking, pushups, and pull-ups, you never have to go inside a gym. Of course you would have to get some sort of pull-up bar. Even with pushups alone, you can change your physique, especially with a good, healthy diet. While pushups are free, and other strength exercises can be near to free, if you have a set of dumbbells, a bench, and a pushup bar, still get a gym membership because it is good for you to get out of your home and be around other health-conscious people. I do not think that isolation is healthy and getting yourself to the gym every morning, noon, or evening is going to help motivate you into taking positive actions for your health every day. Pushups will enable you to build a stronger body as pushups are a full body exercise. You will have the experience of 'working the field' when you are doing pushups, but for the maximum effect I chose to incorporate two more weight lifting exercises, the deadlift, and the squat.

If you told me one day I would be doing deadlifts and squats, I would have thought you were out of your mind, or I was. I have discovered something that bodybuilders have known for decades: these two exercises are about the best you can do for total body conditioning.

With squats, you can start with no weight. For deadlifts, you can start with no weight or small dumbbells or a barbell that you might have lying in your basement or garage. Join a gym so you can have access to good and safe equipment, and if the gym membership replaces your medication costs, it will be well worth it.

Let us take a look at both the deadlift and the squat for the last two exercises to "work your field" with. They are both incredibly powerful.

Action Plan

Start doing pushups today. Start with one if you cannot do more, and gradually add on until you reach your goal of one hundred pushups straight. That is a goal as lofty as climbing Mount Everest, but keep on the path of getting stronger and you will get there. I have not reached that goal either, so this way we will keep doing pushups till we do.

LESSONS OF THE VINEYARD

WORKING YOUR FIELD WITH DEADLIFTS

Here are some reasons to start deadlifting today:

1. Lift yourself out of depression. The benefits of doing deadlifts extend beyond the body and even to your mood and confidence.
2. The muscular benefits of deadlifts are more powerful than just about any other exercise besides squats.
3. There are benefits of deadlifts for women as well. The idea that deadlifts are for men only is not accurate. Women should not be concerned about bulking up; they will get lean as they do not have enough testosterone to become bulky.
4. Melt your belly fat. Before deadlifts, I had what appeared to be a pregnant belly, 250 pounds and a forty-eight-inch waist. After I had started deadlifting consistently, the benefits of deadlifts began to appear: improved mood, melted belly fat, 175 pounds, thirty-two-inch waist.
5. Deadlifts are not just for bodybuilders, powerlifters, and athletes, but doing deadlifts can help you look and feel like an athlete, or at least like a normal person again.
6. The health benefits of deadlifts are for any age, even into your nineties! Deadlifts when done with proper form are that safe.
7. Deadlifts are great for people who have little time to exercise.
8. The muscular benefits of deadlifts happen gradually with amazing gains.

9. The deadlift is the king of exercise because you practically engage your entire muscle mass with one movement. Stop wasting your time just doing biceps and wrist curls.

10. The benefits of deadlifts for weight loss are overlooked. Start deadlifting, stop dieting, and watch the pounds melt away. This is a nice by-product of deadlifting to deal with depression.

11. Deadlifts build your grip strength.

12. Deadlifting can build a great physique no matter what your shape is now and no matter what your age is.

13. Deadlifts will improve your posture.

14. The benefits from deadlifts cover the major muscle groups.

15. Deadlifts benefit your core, giving you that lean defined waist and the abs you thought are only for Hollywood.

16. Deadlift benefits for women include sculpting the posterior more than just about any other exercise, other than squats.

17. Deadlift benefits for men include boosting testosterone. Raising testosterone is a significant weapon in the battle against depression.

18. Proper form deadlifts are safe.

19. Deadlifts lessen back pain and prevent injury.

20. Deadlifts have real-world application whenever you have to lift heavy things like an air conditioner, couch, TV, or heavy suitcase.

21. Deadlifts can be an excellent cardiovascular conditioner.

22. Deadlifting requires very little equipment; you do not have to build yourself a swimming pool.

23. Deadlifts are a true measure of strength with one specific movement that almost anyone can do.

24. Deadlifting is a very primal movement and can generate a great sense of physical power as well as mind power that is critical for dealing with depression.

The deadlift is a great tool in your arsenal to battle depression. Just about every muscle in your body will be engaged while doing deadlifts. This applies to people who do not experience depression, and surprisingly to those who do. Many people who are depressed think that sitting around and sulking over the sad thoughts that race through their mind is about the best they can do for their depression, along with popping a few antidepressants. There is another way to fight depression, whether your depression is thought based and/or chemical.

According to the National Institute of Mental Health, an estimated 26.2 percent of Americans ages eighteen and older—about one in four adults—suffer from a diagnosable mental disorder in a given year. When applied to the 2004 U.S. Census residential population estimate for ages eighteen and older, this figure translates to 57.7 million people, and is higher in 2015.

We are not alone, we are among the 26% who struggle with depression. Starting a strength-training program that includes deadlifting can literally change your life.

I cannot guarantee that you will not need medications. You should defer to your doctor, but there is a good chance that you can manage your depression symptoms with real food and full-body exercise, perhaps as well as with medication. The only side effects in the case of not using medication will be losing body fat, building muscle, and getting a lean and trim body. Deadlift benefits can include relief from depression when done consistently.

There are two reasons deadlifts can offer potential relief from depression. The first is the sheer total body strength requirement. Deadlifts have a known effect on hormones, and raising testosterone and endorphins that are going to improve your mood. The second is metaphorical, inspirational, and motivational. When you experience yourself deadlifting heavy weight, it is easier to imagine that you can deal with whatever stresses and weights you have on your mind. The same way that you will build muscle to accomplish the deadlift, you be able to handle the mental and/or emotional weights that have been keeping you mired in depression. You will be filled with more confidence, inspiration, and motivation to overcome the challenges that you are facing in your life.

How to safely perform the deadlift: Warm up for at least five minutes. A good walk outside, on the treadmill, or on the elliptical should do the trick to break a little sweat. Then, start out with an Olympic-size bar and 2.5lb plates on either side, just so that the bar is raised enough so you can get a grip. This is fifty pounds of weight. If this is too heavy, then you will start with lighter dumbbells, but I am assuming that you can lift a fifty-pound bar. If you don't have equipment or do not want to join a gym, all you need are a few pieces of great equipment to set up a home gym for deadlifting to start, an Olympic barbell and plates which you might already have in your basement or garage.

Keep your feet shoulder width; put your left hand and your right hand on the bar in an overhand position. There are people who use an underhand grip with one of their hands, but for now, especially with a light weight, you should be able to start out with an overhand grip. Keep your back straight. Look at a fixed point on the floor or wall in front of you. Take a firm grip on the bar. Keep your hips low. Take a deep breath and tighten your core. If you watch experienced lifters, you will see that they hold their breath through the deadlift as well as the squat. Keep your back straight and pick the weight up off the floor. Drive with your legs, not with your back.

Do not lean back when you get to the top. Do not lean back. Then lower the weight.

You can do one repetition of the same weight five times straight or five sets of increasing weight using one repetition, which is what I prefer these days. The deadlift is going to help transform your body and mind. Three times a week is definitely enough, even once a week, but do not forget the feeling that you have of being able to lift the physical weight and how that applies to you also being able to lift the depression off yourself. Make a commitment to become stronger in mind and body.

Instead of spending money to wallow in your misery, whatever the drug of choice is, whether it is drugs, alcohol, cigarettes, junk food, or antidepressants that are not helping you, spend your money to get healthy with some gym equipment and/or a gym membership, walking, pushups, and now deadlifts.

You can walk every day, or five times a week. Pushups you can do three to five times a week. Deadlifts and squats are for three times a week or once a week. They are that powerful. You might not be able to walk at all after your first set of squats or deadlifts, as you will be stressing muscles that might not have been used for decades. Do not give up; just keep progressing gradually, one day at a time.

Action Plan

Start a deadlift workout program as soon as you are ready. Becoming ready to deadlift might require some prerequisite time as in losing weight if you are obese. As with all the other exercises that I speak of to fight depression, especially deadlifting, squats, pushups, and running, you should not begin training until you have your doctor's approval.

LESSONS OF THE VINEYARD

WORKING YOUR FIELD
WITH SQUATS

Squats are known as the king of free-weight exercises. The squat is another exercise that can help to alleviate depression and change your physique. Begin with no weight and do what is called air squats. Build up slowly to squat using weights, starting with just the forty-five-pound Olympic bar. Keep increasing in weight from there. Start with one set of five repetitions once you are using weight, every other day with weekends off. If you like to do multiple sets, do five sets of five repetitions. I cannot guarantee immediate results from the first workout, but I am pretty sure that you will feel the effects. You will probably be a little sore, but rest up and keep squatting. Soon, the results of doing the squats will speak for themselves.

You will be able to cope better with your depression. You might even feel total relief from your depression. The physical movement of having a very heavy weight on your shoulders and being able to stand up straight despite the challenge of the weight will help you visualize doing the same with the other burdens that you are carrying on your shoulders. "Just as I can lift this weight, I can deal with my depression" is something you can say and experience.

I read up on building muscle in general and everywhere I looked, squats were touted as the king of all exercises. I was not too happy to hear that because I have a torn medial meniscus in my left knee, and I was frankly terrified of doing squats. But based on many articles, I was confident that if I used proper form, specifically squatting so my hips were slightly below parallel to my knees, I would not only be okay, but I would increase strength in my legs, overall body, and even knees. And that is exactly what has happened since I began doing squats.

There is a big difference between a leg press in a machine and a squat. In the leg press, I felt like an astronaut, lying on the beach with my coconut water in one hand and then pushing the weights with little effort, as the machine seems to be doing a lot of the work and the support. With free-weight squats, that is not the case. You have to stabilize the weight on your shoulder, which takes effort as the poundage goes up. Then you have to squat down correctly with good form and get back up. You can feel your entire body engaged in the squat.

Is the squat hard? Yes. Is the squat more difficult than other exercises you have done? Yes. Are the benefits of squats real? Yes. Is it worth taking up the squat? Absolutely. Here are my reasons why squats are an awesome way to "work your field," to break up the dirt and get ready for building a better life:

Time needed for squats: If all I did in the gym was squats, I'd feel like I had accomplished something. A session of squats can be done in thirty to forty-five minutes, if not faster. You can dare yourself to do squats. For many years I went to the gym and did the machines, shoulder press, leg press, leg curl, but nothing had the type of impact on my body and mental state as squatting.

No other exercises gave me the same depression relief as squats, deadlifts, pushups, and walking/elliptical/swimming. It is true that I was not eating real food daily at that time, so that could be a very big factor, but nonetheless, I believe that just the squat, deadlift, pushup, and walking will have a huge impact on how you feel. What is the point of all those machine exercises without actual change to your mind and body?

Who wants to spend time in the gym if it is not beneficial to your mind and body? Is there a purpose to just going to the gym without seeing results? I want big changes. I had tried over ten different antidepressants with catastrophic side effects. I wanted to find some way out of the hell of depression. I am sure that you do too. I can see the big changes from squats. I can see the benefits of squats; I can see the benefits of deadlifts. I could not see many benefits from machines. One of the key benefits of squats is that it reduces the amount of time that you have to spend working out. Do the core exercises like squats, deadlifts, and pushups and forget the rest that are not transforming your mind and body the way you want.

The effectiveness of the squat: For the time invested, squats are incredibly effective. I know that squats are harder and less comfortable to do, but that is the point. Do them safely and reap the benefits of squats. It is a challenge to do squats, but they are just too transformative and powerful not to incorporate them into your workout.

Squats can build your knee strength: I believe that my legs are stronger today because of squats, including my knees. As I mentioned, I have a torn medial meniscus and was terrified of doing squats, but I have been doing them as suggested, going below parallel, and have been pleasantly surprised that my legs overall are stronger.

Squats are a perfect teacher of gradual improvement: Squats are great for gradual improvement. Every week you can go up by 2.5 or 5 pounds.

Milo of Croton was a sixty-century BC wrestler who enjoyed a brilliant wrestling career and won many victories in the most important athletic festivals of ancient Greece. In addition to his athletic victories, Milo is credited by the ancient commentator Diodorus Siculus with leading his fellow citizens to military triumph over neighboring Sybaris in 510 BC. Like other successful athletes of ancient Greece, Milo was the subject of fantastic tales of strength and power, some, perhaps, based upon misinterpretations of statues dedicated to his likeness. Among other tales, he was said to have carried a bull on his shoulders.[29]

As the story goes, to achieve this strength, Milo began lifting a young bull. He continued to do this every day, and as the bull gradually grew

29 https://en.wikipedia.org/wiki/Milo_of_Croton

in size, Milo gained strength to match. This story of Milo illustrates the idea of gradual improvement, which is central to strength training. Most of us need to accept where we are today and then work toward a goal step by step. If we are consistent, we will reach it. For every five- or ten-pound increase in squats, you will see the change in your body, everywhere. Challenge yourself to grow stronger with squats.

The squat builds emotional strength to fight depression: One of the chief benefits of squats is the emotional strength that you get from doing them. As you get physically stronger, when you see that you are increasing your physical strength, this can give you additional confidence to move forward, against and through whatever emotional challenges you might be facing. Being stronger in your body will help you be stronger in your mind.

"When your shoulders are loaded with heavy physical weight, and you can lift it, this will give you the confidence that you can lift other burdens off your shoulders, even if they seem too heavy to deal with. For more inspiration on how to build more muscle and become a better athlete with one of the best moves in fitness, read an article called 7 Reasons to Never Neglect Squats[30] It was written by Jeremey DuVall and details the benefits of squats, including how they stimulate muscle-building hormones. They also involve almost every muscle in the body. Strengthening muscles using squats will also help you avoid injury when running or jumping.

"I want to share with you the top eight benefits of squats as suggested by Dr. Mercola, with my additional comments.

"The Squat Builds Muscle in Your Entire Body - Squats obviously help to build your leg muscles (including your quadriceps, hamstrings, and calves), but they also create an anabolic environment, which promotes body-wide muscle building. In fact, when done properly, squats are so

---

30 http://www.mensfitness.com/training/build-muscle/
get-stronger-7-reasons-never-neglect-squats

intense that they trigger the release of testosterone and human growth hormone in your body, which are vital for muscle growth and will also help to improve muscle mass when you train other areas of your body aside from your legs. "I should mention here that my testosterone levels have doubled since I started to squat."

"Functional Exercise Makes Real-Life Activities Easier - Functional exercises are those that help your body to perform real-life activities, as opposed to simply being able to operate pieces of gym equipment. Squats are one of the best functional exercises out there, as humans have been squatting since the hunter-gatherer days. When you perform squats, you build muscle and help your muscles work more efficiently, as well as promote mobility and balance. All of these benefits translate into your body moving more efficiently in the real world. "I feel that walking around the city is easier, my legs are stronger, going up stairs is easier, my entire body feels more conditioned since I began doing squats."

"The Squat Burns More Fat - One of the most time-efficient ways to burn more calories is actually to gain more muscle! For every pound of additional muscle you gain, your body will burn an additional 50-70 calories per day. If you gain 10 pounds of muscle, you will automatically burn 500-700 more calories per day than you did before. "My fat percentage decreased by 3%, from 22% to 19% over six months." The main change I had made during that period had been heavier lifting, especially with squats and deadlifts.

"Maintain Mobility and Balance - Strong legs are crucial for staying mobile as you get older, and squats are phenomenal for increasing leg strength. They also work out your core, stabilizing muscles, which will help you to maintain balance, while also improving the communication between your brain and your muscle groups, which helps prevent falls—which is incidentally the #1 way to prevent bone fractures versus consuming mega-dose calcium supplements and bone drugs.

"Prevent Injuries - Most athletic injuries involve weak stabilizer muscles, ligaments and connective tissues, which squats help strengthen.

Squats also help prevent injury by improving your flexibility (squats improve the range of motion in your ankles and hips) and balance, as noted above.

"Sports Performance Jump Higher and Run Faster - Whether you are a weekend warrior or a mom who chases after a toddler, you will be interested to know that studies have linked squatting strength with athletic ability. Specifically, squatting helped athletes run faster and jump higher, which is why this exercise is part of virtually every professional athlete's training program.

"The Squat Tones Your Backside, Abs and Entire Body - Few exercises work as many muscles as the squat, so it is an excellent multipurpose activity useful for toning and tightening your behind, abs, and, of course, your legs. Furthermore, squats build your muscles, and these muscles participate in the regulation of glucose and lipid metabolism and insulin sensitivity, helping to protect you against obesity, diabetes and cardiovascular disease.

"Help with Waste Removal - Squats improve the pumping of body fluids, aiding in the removal of waste and delivery of nutrition to all tissues, including organs and glands. They are also useful for the improved movement of feces through your colon and more regular bowel movements."[31]

What is the proper way to do squats?

You better find out before you start do squat. Even though the squat is one of the most powerful exercises for your entire body, the squat can also be one of the most dangerous, if you do not learn the **proper way to do squats** and keep practicing perfect technique. Start with just your body weight and go up gradually in weight on the bar. Do not be a fool

---

31 http://fitness.mercola.com/sites/fitness/archive/2012/05/25/darin-steen-
demonstrates-the-perfect-squat.aspx

and endanger your body. You must internalize the proper way to do squats, in your mind and in your body.

Proper Way to do Squats - Warmup

Do at least 5 warm up sets, 5 reps, 4 reps, 3 reps, 2 reps and 1 rep - each set using a bit heavier weight till you are ready for your work set.

For example, if you are going to do a squat workout with 100 pounds, warm up with:

45lbs for 5 reps,

65 pounds for 4 reps,

85lbs for 3 reps,

90 pounds for 2 reps and

95lbs for 1 rep

At that point, you are ready to do your five work sets of five repetitions with 100 pounds. Before your squat workout with weights, make sure to do some practice squats with great form without weights.

Proper Way to do Squats - The Commandments

Here are the most important guidelines for the *proper way to do squats*:

1. Do not hold the barbell with your hands as much as with your back.
2. Put the bar right above your traps, a bit below your shoulders, without using any padding so you can feel the weight of the bar.
3. The bar's weight should be on your body, not on your hands or wrists, so best to keep your thumb above the bar instead of underneath.
4. Start with light weight and just the bar itself is fine.
5. Feel the bar's weight on your shoulders and not on your wrists.
6. Feel that bar's weight to be directly over the middle of your foot.

7. Keep your feet at your heels about shoulder width from each other.

8. Point your toes out at about 11 am and 1 pm on a clock or about 30 degrees.

9. Keep your head down a bit looking towards a point low on the wall in front of you.

10. Don't admire your self in the mirror, that means that you are holding your head to high.

11. When you start your descent in the squat, make sure that your knees are pushing outwards.

12. Keep your knees above your toes.

13. Feel your rear lowering below the top of your knees and think of yourself as you are going to bounce back up from the lowest position using the muscles of your tuchas, aka rear end, aka as your posterior chain.

14. Your descent should be controlled.

15. When your rear end hits below parallel, think of your butt being pulled up straight to the ceiling.

16. You should not feel like you are pushing hard with your feet against the floor.

17. You should not feel as if you are struggling with your upper body to lift up the weight in the squat.

18. You should not feel as if your knees are absorbing all of the weight and have all the pressure to power up the weight.

19. You should feel as if it is your posterior chain, your rear that is powering you back up.

The big proper way to do the squat secret is in focusing on using your rear end muscles to power the lift.

I have erred in the past because I never thought of those muscles and was not aware that is where I should be driving from.

20. Feel as if you are driving up the weight vertically using the power in your posterior chain.

21. Feel as if you are moving the weight perfectly vertical down and up.

22. Make sure to take a deep breath in before beginning your descent and keep holding your breath until you are standing again.

23. If you do the squat this way, your knees should feel more like a joint that your legs are gliding around, rather than the prime mover of the weight.

24. Before you begin your descent, make sure that your chest is up.

25. Your body should be straight, head neutral, looking a bit down, lowering the weight and elevating in a perfect straight line with the middle of your foot.

26. Do 3 to 5 sets of 5 reps with your workset weight. You can choose to go up 5 lbs every workout or 5lbs every week, your choice till you get to heavier weights. Never sacrifice good form for higher weights.[32]

Action Plan

Start a squat program today. Begin with air squats, squats with no weights, and build up from there. Respect the squat and its ability to build a more powerful you, as well as the fact that you must continue to be a student of great form and increase weight gradually, because as much as the squat can build, performing squats incorrectly can have damaging results. So be careful!

---

32 http://hashimashi.com/proper-way-to-do-squats-26-secrets-for-the-perfect-squat/

LESSONS OF THE VINEYARD

WORKING YOUR FIELD
SUMMARY

I have suggested four simple, practical, and effective strategies to work our field, to get our bodies moving, and get the right type of exercise that can help both our body and our mind.

✓ Walking
✓ Pushups
✓ Deadlifts
✓ Squats

Before moving to the next section, here is one more article to motivate you to get moving and "work your field." I read a good article that discusses how a good workout can help you work off depression. It describes how working out makes you feel better and puts you in a better mood. And if you work out regularly, your depression is less likely to return. Many studies show that regular exercise can be, for many, at least as beneficial as medication.[33]

"Researchers at Duke University studied people suffering from depression for 4 months and found that 60% of the participants who weight trained for 40 minutes, 4 times a week overcame their depression

---

33 This article was first printed in the December 2005 issue of the Harvard Mental Health Letter. For more information or to order, please go to http://www.health. harvard.edu/mental

without using antidepressant medication. This is the same percentage rate as for those who only used medication in their treatment for depression."[34]

I said to Joseph, "Those are some hefty results, essentially the same effectiveness from weight training and/or aerobic exercise to overcome depression without using antidepressant medication. If this is not motivation to start moving and doing basic strength training, I do not know what is.

"Wouldn't you rather workout and look better than taking meds and risk their negative side effects? I have done both and I vote for the big four physical activities of walking, pushups, squats, and deadlifts. Of course those are not the only ways to get in a great workout and if you have other exercises that you prefer, go for it, but get started somewhere and keep at it.

You might never need an antidepressant again."

Joseph responded, "I never realized that walking or doing exercise could have an impact on my depression."

"All you have to do is get outside or join a gym."

"I don't know. I have to think about it. Maybe I can start with walking, we will see. In any case though, tell me some more lessons from the vineyard. I am surprised that you came up with these in the first place; making the choice to stop depression, selecting a location with bright sunlight meaning 'bright' thoughts and a physical smile, and this last one, working the ground by uprooting bad memories, burying them, and physically working on our body, our ground, our field. I am just not sure any will apply to me because I believe that my depression is more chemical as opposed to indulging in negative thinking."

"All the more why exercise and a better diet can help you," I replied. "Every morsel of food that you eat, think of it as a drug, a tastier drug

---

34 http://www.bodybuilding.com/fun/fighting_depression.htm

than Seroquel or Neurontin, and every repetition of exercise that you do, all of the above is going to affect the state of chemistry within your body.

"Antidepressants are attempting to promote a healthier biochemistry and you can do the same with food and exercise. You might still need antidepressants, but why not see if you can improve your biochemistry in additional ways like what you eat and how you move your body that will not leave you with dry mouth, no energy, and other potential negative side effects?"

"Granted, I have a lot to think about," said Joseph, "but tell me some of the other lessons of the vineyard in the meantime because I am not stopping my meds at this point and I have no strength to work out. In terms of food, I will try to start adjusting my diet."

LESSONS OF THE VINEYARD

PLANTING THE FIELD

"Is it really accurate to think of a person as a field? Where do we see any evidence for that?" Joseph asked.

"We are using the field as a metaphor for life, but I think that even linguistically we can see that it is not so out there to think of a person as a field. When I was originally struck by the thought of a field as a metaphor, it occurred to me that in the Biblical account of the first man, we are told that he was formed out of the ground and therefore he was named Adam. In Hebrew the word for earth is Adamah.[35] Apparently, the idea of a person being compared to the earth is not a new one. I understand that the original Adam was both a man and a woman before being separated into two distinct beings and their name was Adam to remind them of their essential nature. The name Adam therefore reminds a person that his/her qualities and characteristics have similarities to the earth, or are exactly identical to that of the earth."

"I don't know where you come up with this stuff, but go on."

"For example, just as a field needs intention, sunlight, plowing, and planting of the right seeds to transform the dust of the earth into usable produce, so too does a person need similar actions to become a productive human being.

"It is interesting that there is a direct correlation between the word for *ground* and the word for *person* in Hebrew, Adamah and Adam. Even

---

35 Genesis Chapter 2:Verse 7; Chapter 5:Verses 1–5.

in the English language, which is rooted in Latin, the same connection exists. You thought that hummus is just the name of a Middle Eastern appetizer made out of chickpeas? The Latin word for earth and ground is *humus* and is the origin of many English words that we use daily without realizing their direct link to the ground. Watch how *Humus* progresses to Human."

1. Humus : HUM us (hyu' mus) n. - Earth; ground
2. Humanities : HUMAN ities (hyu man' i teze) n. - Studies and interests of a cultural type which enrich the spirit of mankind
3. Humble : HUM ble (hum' b'l) adj. - Lowly; unpretentious; as, a humble person
4. Human : HUMAN (hyu' man) adj. - of, relating to, or characteristic of people or human beings.
5. Humane : HUMAN e (hyu mane') adj. - Marked by compassion for other human beings and animals
6. Inhuman : in HUMAN (in hyu' man) adj. - Lacking the qualities of a humane being
7. Humanity : HUMAN ity (hyu man' it ee) n. - The quality of being human[36]

"Clearly, in both Hebrew, Latin and English, there is a direct connection between a person and the earth."

"So what," Joseph said. "What does that have to do with depression?"

"If you want to know how to get out of depression, the fastest way is to examine the steps you have to take to turn a depressed vacant field into a lush garden or an award-winning vineyard. The step of planting and sowing seeds is akin to the thoughts that we plant in our mind. Planting a thought is like planting a seed. Eventually that seed will grow and manifest itself into reality.

---

36 http://www.english-for-students.com/human.html

If you think you can do something or you can't, you are right.[37] Our thoughts are the fourth step to creating a better life for us. Our thoughts brought us to the state of depression and it is our thoughts that can bring us out. Even if you say, no, it was not your thoughts that made you depressed, I believe it was the shock waves that hit you in your life that you told me about over the last few months; for example when you saw the numbers of the concentration camp tattooed on your mother's forearm as a boy of eight, when you saved a drowning man and his face appeared in your nightmares at thirteen, when you were held up in a store and threatened with death at only eighteen and losing your father in a car crash."

"Those are all true Benjamin, but the straw that broke the camel's back was when I was served with divorce papers and realized that my children were gradually becoming estranged from me. That last one of estrangement was the final wave where I could not keep my head above water, where I drowned in the flood of my own depression."

The reality is that there are many people that might experience similar tragedies in their lives and they do not fall into depression; for instance, people who have parents that are war refugees or they (themselves) are refugees. There are other people who are involved in accidents or natural disasters, people who are victims of assault and robbery. Practically half the country is divorced and many of the divorcees were shocked to receive divorce papers. While family estrangements are not that common, they do happen.

The question is, why do some of us react with depression to the same events that another person might be able to brush off or deal with in a less self-destructive manner? One idea that has occurred to me repeatedly as I examined my own reactions to the waves in my life that turned into a flood of depression is that it is not what happened which hurt me as much as the way I thought about the event. I realized I would

---

37 http://www.brainyquote.com/quotes/authors/h/henry_ford.html

interpret events in the most negative way possible and then roll that thought around in my mind continuously until what was just a small snowball turned into Mount Everest, and very few people can conquer such a mountain.

No one can judge another's reactions and it is possible that in the future, science will uncover that people are genetically predisposed or locked into depressive traits. However, until that time, it is just my suggestion that if you want to use some weapons to fight depression that cost nothing and are literally all in your mind, start thinking differently.

Start focusing on events that are under your control and not on events that have happened in the past or thoughts that cause you the most pain. Stop reviewing in your mind the scenes that dampen your spirits. Focus on those ideas and goals that will lift your spirits. Get out of the "room of depression" which is essentially our own mind and, for the depressed person, more often than not appears to be the only room.

The ROD is not the movie house you want to be entertained in. I know that I spent way too long in that room of depression before I discovered that I could visually leave and take actions that would prevent me from wanting to go back to my own movies again, despite the tickets being free and available 24 hours a day, 365 days a year.

I believe that we each have our own unique room of depression where we review our own movies, those scenes that upset us, thoughts that sadden, hurt, demoralize, and eventually leave us depressed, sitting in the one chair of the theater surrounded by candy wrappers, popcorn, ice cream, and hot dogs, as none of our family or friends want to be in that theater with us. It is not a fun place to be, for them or for us. Planting a new field means you start thinking of new ways to build new rooms in your mind, a virtual castle if you will, as large as you can make it.

By building new virtual spaces in your mind, you are allowing yourself the flexibility to leave that one room of depression and start to focus on new thoughts, goals, and interests. You are allowing yourself to move forward in your life, beyond the pain that has hampered you up till now, that has kept you isolated in that one lonely room of depression.

"However," I said to Joseph, "before you can start construction on new rooms (a new life), you must get out of your room of depression, lock the door, and do your best to not re-enter. Whatever the great films of the past that are playing there, you have already seen them a million times before, shut them down, get out of that room of depression, and then you can start working on a new film."

"Sounds great," said Joseph, "but how do I get out? Where are the exit doors? How do I exit the room of depression? I have been here a very long time and am used to it. At this point I know little else. Plus what if my depression is purely chemical?"

"You might say that your depression is purely chemical, but when you speak to me, it seems to be more than chemical. Of course there might be chemical underpinnings, but every time we speak, you relate stories of the past, how they hurt and weakened you, and you say that you did not reach this level of depression until you experienced the most troubling of all the stories, the estrangement from your children. While you might have a genetic predisposition to depression, a chemistry that is vulnerable to depression, I still think it is your stories of despair that help to trigger the depression. Now, if you say that because you are so weak that you cannot take any action, you yourself agree that you have experienced this weakness and physical exhaustion after you started your medications. So this is how I see it. You need to exit the room of depression, the spark that fires up your chemical weakness, and at the same time, strengthen your physical body and biochemistry to fend off the sparks of depression.

"What is the room of depression?" I continued. "It is that space where you have been spending an inordinate amount of time that you might even cause distance between yourself, friends, and family."

"My family has nothing to do with me. I do not exist for them. I have been cut out of my own life. I do not even know who I am, where I am, if I am even alive. It seems like a total—"

"Calm down, please, the loss of your family is not even the worst."

"Oh really, what can be worse than that?"

"I believe that the distance living in the room of depression causes between you and yourself is the most severe."

"I never thought about that, between me and myself, what does that even mean?"

"You just said it. You feel like you have been cut out of your own life, as if you do not even exist. You are not even sure if you were ever born, who you are, where you are, what you are doing.

"Everything feels like a nightmare and it is because you have no connection with yourself. Your entire self-worth is wrapped up in the acceptance of other people and you have still not yet approved or accepted yourself.

"By living in that room, whatever the scenes are that you are replaying, whatever the conversations are, whatever your thoughts are, that room is causing you an enormous amount of pain, isolation, and disconnection from your own life. And you are still sitting there? For how long, for how many years can you do that?

"Over time, if you do not leave that room, you will be saturated, and marinated in depressive thoughts which could have catastrophic consequences. The end result might be that you live in that room, focus on events that you have little to no control of, and grow more distant from yourself, your family, and your friends. Is that the life that you want?"

"No. I want out, I am sick of it and sick of myself the way I am right now. How do I get out?"

"Here are two ways. The first is to visually leave that room, close the door, and let all the memories, videos, and conversations remain there. For years, you have had no other room but that place. You have to move out. The other way is physically. Stop sitting, moping, and sulking. Physically, start walking, moving, and taking action.

"Now that you have visualized yourself leaving the room of depression, shut and lock the door. It is tempting, after years of living there, to want to go back. That is natural. But you must lock the door. When you lock it in your mind, you will have some space to create anew, which will enable you to focus on the third way by building new virtual rooms."

"Virtual room?" Joseph repeated. "Are you in space, what planet are you from? What is a virtual room?"

"A virtual room is a place in your mind, a space where you visualize yourself building a room that will make you more productive by focusing on and improving yourself. For me, it was to focus on learning additional technical skills; writing, losing weight, walking, pushups, weight training, and better nutrition. For you, it might be excelling in your career, paying more attention to your loved ones, friends, a language, music, losing weight, building strength—all are productive and valuable 'home improvement projects.'"

"Home improvement projects? Fields, ground, trees, and now home. These metaphors are supposed to get me out of depression?"

"I do not want to burst your bubble, but if you think mocking my metaphors makes you feel better, fine. You are the one who is unemployed, You are the one who has no family connections. You are the one not invited to your own child's wedding, who has been isolated and living in solitary confinement for over a decade. If you do not want to try anything new, no problem. If you think that your life is just fine and dandy the way it is, no problem. It is all up to you, your choice, we can stop right here."

Joseph was silent for a few minutes. I did not know if that was the end of our conversation. He just kept staring straight ahead, not saying anything. He was frozen in thought as every sentence I said penetrated deeper. I did not mean to hurt him, but I wanted him to see things accurately. Finally he spoke.

"You are right, I am not proud of where I am or what I have become. Let me hear the rest of the metaphors from the vineyard and I have to see if any can help or resonate with me."

"So we were talking about building new rooms, a new home. Now that you have left and locked the door of the ROD, you can focus on building your new virtual home. Make it a palace, a mansion, make it spectacular, and make it a paradise. I know that at some point in this process, you will feel excited by whatever you are creating.

"People want to be productive by nature. Just as the earth produces, we also want to produce. We want to contribute to our families, the world, and ourselves. Once you get out of that room of depression, you are going to be able to focus on your new home and love living in it. Strengthen these rooms by thinking about new interests, making goals related to your new rooms, celebrating the progress that you are making day by day, and never go back to the room of depression.

"The more you strengthen your new rooms with positive thoughts, the less likely it will be that you re-enter the room of depression. The more you think about your new life and new activities, the happier you will be. The closer you get to your new goals, the more productive you will feel. This is how you plant a new vineyard and start to build a new life. This is how you can put the brakes on your depression and begin constructing a new home for yourself visually. If you do leave your room of depression and begin working on new thoughts, plans, ideas, and goals, you can experience relief from the depression that is caused by sitting in the room of depression.

"The memories that give you pain will most likely never disappear. However, you can start to put distance between you and the constant thoughts that you once spent much of the day thinking about when you leave your room of depression.

"You will be building a new home. Instead of having a one-room home, you will create a palace. The one room might still be there, but it will be in the basement, locked and not frequented because you will be too busy in the rest of the rooms of your house. The second way to think of it is from a musical point of view.

"Imagine that you hear a musician playing one note, all the time, with no end in sight. Who wants to hear such a "song"? When we have the same thoughts of depression over and over, it is very similar to a one-note song, a one-dimensional person. Good songs use many notes on the scale, and a richer and fuller life is going to exist outside of the one room of painful memories and thoughts. Planting new thoughts in your mind to build a richer and fuller life is a great way to use the powerful teachings of relationship between the qualities of the earth and yourself, the lessons of the vineyard."

Action Plan

Plant new ways of thinking in order to produce the best wine out of your life. We reap what we plant, so make the plantings count.

LESSONS OF THE VINEYARD

WATERING THE FIELD

"Watering the field," Joseph said to me, "is about giving nourishment to the field, a metaphor to changing eating habits from junk food to good food to support the growth of healthy tissue in the body and brain?"

"Now you are the one who is drawing out the lessons and creating metaphors," I said. "Every crop needs a good source of water to grow, especially grapes. The same is true for us. We need more than good thoughts, we need good physical nourishment in order to grow and flourish. In the last lesson of planting the field, we spoke about the need to think right, to focus our thoughts on that which we can control and on positive goals. We compared the process of planting thoughts in our head to that of planting seeds in a field. The seeds we plant will become the fruits of that field, so too the thoughts we plant in our mind will turn into the reality that we live in.

"In this lesson, we will go beyond the sowing stage where the seeds have been planted, where we are thinking right and focused on positive thoughts and goals. A field needs real physical nourishment, mainly in the form of water for the planted seeds to develop; so too do we need real healthy and good nourishment to flourish, develop and grow.

"All the good thoughts in the world will be of no use if we are destroying our bodies with food that has no chance of building and/or repairing our cells. Your body will thrive and even transform from feeding yourself healthy food, and so will your brain. We know that the brain needs healthy food to function as much as you need energy to run a marathon or just get by during the day. Start to feed your body real food and you will also be giving yourself the best chance to strengthen the cells of your brain, which helps you in beating depression. What does good nourishment for your body and your mind look like? An Oreo or an apple?"

"Well, having grown up on Oreos, I would much prefer Oreos and milk over apples. However, that is probably the problem. I spent the majority of my most formative years eating processed foods. When I was a kid, I thought that carrots and peas grew in aluminum foil because the only place I saw them was in a compartment of a Swanson fried chicken frozen food tray."

"I would not be surprised if much of the food that you still eat every day is highly processed and resembles little of what you can find in nature."

"That is probably true," Joseph said.

"The first recommendation therefore is to implement the plain meaning of watering your field, meaning to focus on drinking cool, healthy life-giving water. The second will be to target vegetables, whole, real, green vegetables, as the basis for your meals going forward. Eat real food and avoid eating processed foods.

"Rick Nauert, PhD, recommends that individuals need to stay hydrated at all times because even mild dehydration can affect your energy and mood.[38] The takeaway is to stay hydrated by drinking a minimum of eight 8-ounce glasses of water a day or even up to a gallon.

"The site curezone.com published an article which states that while your body is 75% water, your brain tissue is 85% water and needs a sufficient supply of pure water on a daily basis in order to function properly. Depression therefore is a common result of a dehydrated brain.[39]

---

38 http://psychcentral.com/news/2012/02/20/dehydration-influences-mood-cognition/35037.html

39 http://owen.curezone.com/healing/depressiondehydration.html

"Joseph, You mentioned to me that you usually drink soda throughout the day as well as orange juice and coffee in the morning. This is a problem because your body needs additional water to process the soda, juice and coffee. You can actually end up dehydrated and possibly depressed if your body satisfies it's need for water from your brain. You might be unintentionally draining your brain of the water which it needs to function at an optimum level.

"Listen to this quote from "Your Body's Many Cries for Water," by Dr. F. Batmanghelidj, M.D., perhaps the world's most respected expert on our body's need for water: "Pathology that is seen to be associated with 'social stresses'—fear, anxiety, insecurity, persistent emotional and matrimonial problems—and the establishment of depression are the results of water deficiency to the point that the water requirement of brain tissue is affected. The brain uses electrical energy that is generated by the water drive of the energy-generating pumps. With dehydration, the level of energy generation in the brain is decreased.

"Many functions of the brain that depend on this type of energy become inefficient. We recognize this inadequacy of function, and call it depression."

"This is amazing that I can potentially help my depression just by drinking water" Joseph exclaimed.

"Remember that you have to drink between 2 and 4 quarts of water every day. And if you drink other liquids like coffee, juice, alcohol and soda, then you need to drink three to four times the amount of that liquid in water. The lesson of Watering your field is not a metaphor, it is among the simplest of actions that you can take to help ease your depression.

"What about drinking diet soda? Is there any problem with that?" Joseph asked.

"Not only will diet soda require additional water for processing, but diet soda has also been linked to depression in a national institute of health study. According to the research, soda drinkers are 30 percent more likely to be depressed than non-soda drinkers and the risk appeared to be greater for diet soda drinkers.[40]

"So what can I drink if I cannot drink coffee, juice or soda?"

"I am not telling you to never drink coffee, tea or soda. I am telling you to be more conscious of drinking water and to increase the amount of water that you drink every day in order to help your brain operate at an optimum level. Crowd out the coffee, juices and soda, diet or regular by drinking more water, at least eight glasses a day.[41]

"If you find plain water boring, I suggest that you keep a cold quart container of water in your fridge at all times which has some slices of lemon, lime or orange. The cold water is going to help to quench your thirst and the natural flavors of fruit that you like will help you to avoid diet sodas. Another option is green tea with a little honey or stevia for sweetness. Keep in mind that in addition to the benefits of water for your brain, drinking sufficient water and green tea are both known as excellent tools for burning off fat, so you will be helping yourself to fight both depression and obesity at the same time. Fill up and drink your cold quart pitcher of water at least four to five times a day, that can be so much more refreshing to your body and mind than a six pack of diet soda. What have you got to lose other than the weight of depression and obesity?

"I had no clue that the diet soda I drink could be a factor in my depression," Joseph said.

"Think about it, you drink diet soda, yet you are tipping the scales at 275 pounds. There is nothing diet about diet soda. The best drink for you is water and the best types of foods for you are those that grow from the ground: plants and vegetables. There will be plenty to eat, do not worry."

---

40 http://www.usnews.com/news/articles/2013/01/09/
    nih-study-links-soda-with-depression

41 http://health.howstuffworks.com/wellness/food-nutrition/facts/avoid-
    artificialsweeteners.htm

"Okay, so what can or should I eat?"

"For example, instead of having a blueberry muffin or donut in the morning for breakfast, try having some fresh vegetable juice which can flood your body with nutrients instead of sugar and fat. If you need something heavier, then try having a bowl of old-fashioned oatmeal with strawberries and a couple of organic eggs. Instead of having pizza for lunch, try having a baked potato and black bean soup, or a large salad with tuna fish or chicken or brown rice and chicken or beans.

"Instead of having the Swanson's frozen dinner at night that you grew up on, try having quinoa and chickpeas or salmon. Keep it lean and green, making sure to have as many vegetables as you can. Instead of a Snickers bar for a snack, have an apple or a handful of nuts. Eating real food, and not processed, is not complicated, but it is something that most of us are not too used to, so having some clear guidance is welcome. What is good nutrition for a healthy body and mind? Think about eating the foods that are available in nature.

"The foundation of your diet should be vegetables, foods that grow from the ground, as they are most plentiful and loaded with vitamins and micronutrients. The fact that so many different types of vegetables and grains grow from the same earth is in and of itself amazing, different colors, tastes, textures, herbs, and spices. My suggestion to you is that for every main meal of your day, you ensure that you have a healthy amount of vegetables with that meal.

Starting the day off with a tall glass of freshly juiced vegetables like kale, spinach, chard, carrot, beets, apple, lemon and ginger will give you a much needed boost of nutrients that we rarely get in the standard diet most of us have been eating for most of our life. If you have an omelet in the morning, make sure to add vegetables to your omelet, such as onion, garlic, tomato, and/or spinach. If you have rice and chicken in the afternoon, have a side of broccoli or eggplant.

"If you have beans or salmon in the evening, be sure to have a sweet potato or okra. This is simple; just make sure that for every main meal, you eat your vegetables. No matter what diet you have ever read, from Paleo to Atkins to macrobiotics or Weight Watchers, there is no diet that rejects vegetables. Paleo might reject grains, and vegans might reject meat, but everybody agrees to eat vegetables.

"Interestingly enough, the same ancient document that we interpreted in regards to Noah planting a vineyard and why that is a model for us to overcome depression, also states that the primal food of man is green vegetables, plants, any food that has the seed within it like fruits, vegetables and nuts. Going green or eating green is not a brand new idea as you can see here: "I have given you every seed bearing herb, that grows on the earth and every tree that has seed bearing fruit; it will be your food. Everything that moves upon the earth may eat every green herb."[42]

"When I say whole grain, I do not mean wheat bread. I mean whole oats, brown rice, quinoa, baked potato, corn, or sweet potato.

"Even from the previous list of whole grains, out of all of them I would focus on sweet potato or quinoa, but when you are out and about or just super hungry, there is nothing wrong with some oats, brown rice, and corn or baked potato. The best time to have higher carb foods is after a workout when your muscles are hungry for carbs to replace the energy that was expended during your workout without diminishing your existing muscle mass.

"To keep it really simple, Zehhu is the foundation where we say enough to the downward spiral and we commit to finding a way out of depression. The lessons of the vineyard teach us how to make our field productive, where we take action to produce a new version of ourselves in both mind and body. 'Watering the field' encompasses the nutritional component and can be summed up in three words: Eat Real Food.

"Eat real food by definition means to focus on the real foods that we can eat by nature and to avoid, like the plague, as much processed food

---

42 Genesis Chapter 1:29-30

as possible. There are going to be events and times of the year where it will make sense to have some birthday or wedding cake or stuffing with the family on Thanksgiving, but for the most part, stick with real food. Eat real food daily, and lift weights (either weightlifting or your own body weight) to lose fat and build muscle.

That is it. No big secrets, no big special plans or pills. Sure there are supplements that can be beneficial, but the biggest benefit you will see at first will be from real food, real vegetables, fruits, nuts, seeds, and lean protein choices, whether they be plant based like tofu or animal based like eggs and salmon.

"In just sixty days, I dropped over thirty pounds. Almost immediately, during that time, I noticed that the more good food I was eating, the less junk I was craving and the compulsion for the midnight dash for muffins at the deli had disappeared. I could tell that the darkness of constant hunger was being lifted ever so slightly, but enough that I was feeling relief. I did work out as well, but I am sure that the real food I had been eating was the key. So, what is real food? I had to ask myself the same question after having spent a lifetime noshing on Snickers bars and eating macaroni and cheese or chicken pot pie for dinner.

"Real food includes vegetables, fruits, nuts, fish, chicken, eggs, and sometimes yogurt (without added sugars). A moderate amount of sweet potatoes, sometimes a little white potato, and sometimes a little whole grain like quinoa or kasha or oatmeal. I am not a doctor or an expert nutritionist, I am just a person who has been struggling with obesity for way too long and I had enough. It was time to do something different. At the core is the idea that in order to lose body fat and build muscle, I have to start eating real food and get moving.

"The most significant change has been eating real food daily and lifting weights, whether it be my own body weight or lifting barbell weights focusing on deadlifts, squats, bench press, barbell rows, and shoulder presses. Lifting weights is going to help lift your mood besides losing body fat and building muscle. In addition to the physical workout, you need to keep giving your body and mind real food daily so you have the best chance to have a brain functioning at optimum levels, which can lessen or eliminate your stress.

Here is a sample day's menu from the site Hashi Mashi which is dedicated to fighting depression and obesity by eating real food daily and lifting weights.

"Breakfast:

"Four egg whites, greens, onions, spinach, peppers made into an omelet. Serve with hummus and avocado on the side and some olives. If you don't like eggs, have some cottage cheese and melon or plain yogurt with berries and some almonds. If you are doing your workouts in the morning and want a quick boost another option is a high-quality whey or plant based protein shake to help promote muscle synthesis.

"Snack:

"Cherries, blueberries, or strawberries and some almonds or walnuts. Sprinkle some raisins too if you are really hungry.

"Lunch:

"Have chicken soup, or if you are vegetarian maybe a black bean soup, or a chicken salad or turkey salad. Try to overdose on greens as often as possible.

"Keep eating more vegetables like raw peppers, onion, tomato, spinach and cucumbers.

"Snack:

"Have an apple or peach, whatever is juicy and in season.

"Dinner:

"Sweet potato, baked or boiled, wild salmon, broccoli or any other vegetables sautéed in extra virgin olive oil.

"If I, a former cookie monster who thought he could not live without chocolate chip cookies every day, can do it and enjoy real food daily, I am sure you can as well. That is pretty much all that there is to it. Eat real food daily. Lift weights or your body weight. Get moving with walking, elliptical, swimming, or biking. This will absolutely transform your body over a period of six months to a year, and people will notice. You will lose body fat, build muscle, and change the shape of your body and even your face. You can look like a much younger version of the person you are right now, assuming that you have at least twenty pounds of fat to lose, which is generally considered to be the threshold of body re-composition."[43]

"Is processed food really that bad?"

"You have told me that you have been struggling with weight issues for your entire life, correct?"

"Yes," Joseph replied, "and over the last decade, things have gotten worse. It seems that the older I get, the harder it is to lose weight and if I do lose a little weight, then I put it back on even faster. But what does this have to do with depression?"

"Depression and obesity go hand and hand in many cases. I cannot say which comes first, but I guarantee you that if you can get your physical body under better control, you can start to feel better faster.

"Perhaps this is because you are eating healthier, which is reflected in your appearance, and as a result of healthier food choices, your mind is going to function better as well. No matter which comes first it is clear that depression and obesity are linked and it makes a lot of sense to tackle depression from every angle possible, from the way you think as well as from the way you feed yourself.

"There is little in life that you can control other than your thoughts, words, and actions. This is how we want to do battle with depression, with our thoughts, with our words to ourselves and others, and with our actions. Feeding ourselves is about as basic an action as you can imagine. From the time we were babies, we look for food to keep us going. When we grow up and fight depression, many times we look for the wrong food that will give us a fast high, like Oreos or ice cream, to make us feel better from the mental pain in our minds. But we lose the battle because those highly processed foods are only going to give us a temporary fix.

---

43 http://hashimashi.com/real-food-daily/

Then we have to live with extra rolls of fat and poverty in nutrition that we are giving our bodies.

"We are not giving ourselves the nutrients that our mind and body need to win this war against depressive thoughts, words, and actions unless we give ourselves the best fuel possible. Joseph, you have said that you are overweight. Do you wonder whether it is your fault or not? Do you chastise yourself for not having enough willpower to lose weight?

"Are you jealous of people who can have one cookie while you know you cannot stop at one and will instead polish off the whole box? You cannot stop with one slice of cake and instead will finish off the entire cake, and you still will not be satisfied?

"Is carbohydrate addiction a real physiological issue or is it just a manufactured excuse why we cannot stop eating, even when we want to, even when we are not hungry? I came across a new study that shows that brain addiction to fast food processed carbs is real and not a figment of our imagination."

Highly processed carbohydrates can trigger the same brain mechanism associated with substance addiction, say researchers from the New Balance Foundation Obesity Prevention Center at Boston Children's Hospital reported in The American Journal of Clinical Nutrition (June 26th, 2013 issue). In other words, eating high glycemic foods, such as highly processed carbohydrates, can trigger overwhelming hunger and stimulate regions in the brain associated with reward and cravings.

Study leader, David Ludwig, MD, PhD, said cutting down on these high-glycemic foods may help prevent overeating in obese people. Dr. Ludwig and team had set out to determine whether food consumption might be regulated by dopamine-containing pleasure centers in the brain. Ludwig said, "Beyond reward and craving, this part of the brain is also linked to substance abuse and dependence, which raises the question as to whether certain foods might be addictive." Ludwig and colleagues measured levels of blood glucose and hunger, while at the same time using fMRI (functional magnetic resonance imaging) to observe brain activity, and function. They focused on brain activity during the four-hour period after eating, which drives our eating behavior when we next eat. This latest study included 12 obese or overweight participants.

They were given two types of milkshakes, both with the same number of calories, taste and levels of sweetness. However, one contained high-glycemic carbs (carbohydrates) while the other had low-glycemic carbs. After drinking the high-glycemic milkshake, the volunteers experienced the initial "sugar-rush", a surge in blood glucose levels, followed by a steep crash four hours later. The crash in blood sugar levels was accompanied by overwhelming hunger and intense activity within the nucleus accumbens, a region in the brain involved in addictive behaviors.[44]"

"This study demonstrates what many people who have struggled with their weight have known for their entire lives. After they eat high glycemic index types of food, foods that raise their blood sugar levels fast, such as white bread, candy, sugar, they are overcome by overwhelming hunger, which drives them to continue eating even though they are no longer hungry, also known as a binge. This study helps to explain how obesity is not just a failing of willpower. Obesity has real physiological roots, a real source in addiction that is similar to any other type of addiction such as drugs or alcoholism.

"This also explains the cycle of the yo-yo dieter, who takes off weight over a period of months, then takes a bite of cake or bread, pretzels or chips and within months is back at the weight where they started.

Dr. Richard Friedman in the New York Times reports: Dr. Nora Volkow, director of the National Institute on Drug Abuse, has shown in several brain-imaging studies that people addicted to such drugs as cocaine, heroin and alcohol have fewer dopamine receptors in the brain's reward pathways than non-addicts. Dopamine is a neurotransmitter

---

44 Written by Christian Nordqvist. You can see the full article in Medical News Today and it was once hosted at http://www.medicalnewstoday.com/articles/262603.php

critical to the experience of pleasure and desire, and sends a signal to the brain.

This finding and others like it suggest that drug addicts may have blunted reward systems in the brain and that for them, everyday pleasures do not come close to the powerful reward of drugs. There is some intriguing evidence that there is an increase in D2 receptors in addicts who abstain from drugs, though we don't yet know if they fully normalize with time.[45]

"For us this means that genetic variation between individuals, variation between individuals, specifically in the number of their dopamine receptors, might explain why some people become food addicted and obese while others who eat the same foods and grow up in the same envoronment do not."

"So, now what do we do? Let us say that you do not have time in your life for science to prove conclusively that in fact, you do not have the same number of dopamine receptors as your family and friends who cannot understand why you just cannot lose weight.

"Let us say that you do not have time for science to concoct the nanobot technology that will correct or enhance your receptors. Let us say that you do not need a doctor to tell you that after you have highly processed carbs like bagels, white bread, pretzels, chips, candy etc., you also start to feel overwhelming hunger which is incredibly difficult for you to control physiologically and you end up trying to quell the cravings by eating more of those same high-glycemic index foods to give you the jolt of sugar that you need to feel good.

"The answer is fairly simple to state but not necessarily that simple to implement when you factor in socializing to the equation. The answer is to stop doing what you know is harmful to yourself. The answer is to continue socializing, but do not be ashamed that you might have fewer dopamine receptors than your friends or family. This is all genetics. Some

---

45 http://www.nytimes.com/2011/08/02/health/02abuse.html?_r=0

people are tall, some are short, some have a lot of dopamine receptors, and some do not. Whatever gifts nature has blessed us with is nothing for us to gloat about, nor is it something to condemn another person who did not have our good fortune.

"Do what is right for yourself. Stop hiding, do not be ashamed. Socialize, be with your friends and family, but just know that while they might be able to enjoy a slice of Entenmann's awesome pound cake, you cannot, and you should not. Focus on vegetables, low-glycemic fruits, legumes, nuts, some protein, and that is all you have to do. It might take a day or so, maybe more to break the addictive cycle, but hang in there. I have battled the same all my life and can totally understand the frustrations that you have. Do you think that I am exaggerating when I say that processed food can be addictive? How about if I told you that not only can Oreos and the like be addictive, but they can be more addictive than cocaine?"

"That would explain why I can finish a whole box in one sitting," Joseph said.

"Well, while that sounds way out. Look at one more study here which concludes just that."

Study:

Oreos are more addictive than cocaine - A recent study released Wednesday by Connecticut College makes the bold claim that Oreos are as addictive as cocaine — at least, in lab rats.

"You think that is shocking to me? I have been addicted to Oreos since the dawn of my life. But at least I have some confirmation of what I have always felt."

Connecticut College psychology professor Joseph Schroeder told CBS News that rats who ate the high-fat cookies and rats who were exposed to cocaine or morphine had the same pleasure center of their brain stimulated. "When we looked in the pleasure center of the brain, we found that the Oreo cookies activated the pleasure center more so than cocaine would activate the same center," Schroeder said. The study's findings are being used to explain how humans just can't avoid eating high-fat treats, lending credibility to the oft-used saying that "Oreos is so good, it's like crack." A majority of the people polled on CBS News's website agree that Oreos are addictive.

Science blog ZME Science states that Oreos cannot be classified as being more addictive than cocaine because there haven't been enough studies done on people with Oreo withdrawals, highlighting the difference between physiological addiction and psychological addiction.

"In the study, they put rats in a maze and showed that they spent the same amount of time on the side where they were awarded with sugary food compared to the side with not-pleasure (that is bland food) compared to the side of the maze where they were awarded with pleasure (via drugs) vs not-pleasure (that is, not drugs). Interesting, but you can't really go on saying this shows Oreos are like drugs," the ZME Science article states. Yahoo! Health's Prevention blog also claims that other food groups are more addictive than cookies, including chocolate, french fries, candy and ice cream.[46]

"Okay, I get it, I am going to try and do something about my weight problem," said Joseph. "I will try to go for a day or a week, even a month on real food. But I still want to know what fatness has to do with depression."

"First, I can tell you what I experienced with weight loss and how that helped me to cope better with depression. Second, I have also found additional research that has established a link between depression and obesity. This is why I think you should be aware of this link and how that can ultimately help you. Depression and obesity complications are inextricably linked, as you can see in Figure 1."

---

46 Read more: http://dailycaller.com/2013/10/16/
    oreos-more-addictive-than-cocaine/#ixzz2i2GwLYxh

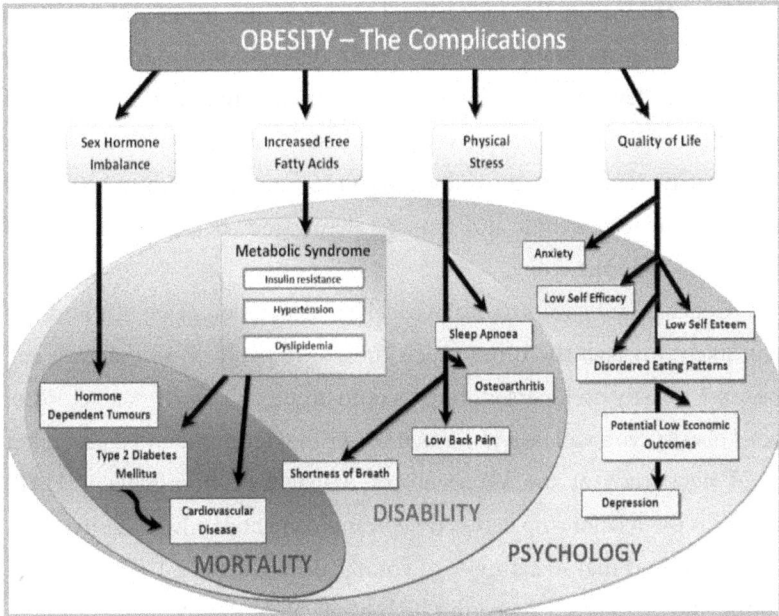

Figure 1 Graphic Credit: http://Healthnewswires.com

"If you are suffering from depression, there is a good chance that you are already overweight or will become overweight. The hormone that links the two is cortisol, a stress hormone that is elevated when there are higher levels of abdominal obesity. This study shows that higher levels of abdominal obesity are directly related to higher levels of depression."

"My waist is already past fifty inches. No wonder I am so depressed."

"Depression and obesity have an unusual marriage. Only one partner gets the public eye and the other is hidden from the masses as much as possible. Successful recovery from obesity is celebrated on just about any major media outlet that you can think of; people are given a hero's welcome when they get rid of their excess fat. I applaud that as well because we all know that not only is that person lighter and more disease resistant, but the people around them are happier. We all feel better around healthy people.

"Depression, on the other hand, is rarely discussed and I cannot think of many celebrated recoveries from depression that are extolled in the media. Nevertheless, depression and obesity are joined at the hip, if not at the waist, and because you have been struggling with depression and obesity, this is the reason I want you to focus on the most powerful strategies to lose weight and manage depression, because you can kill two birds with one stone.

"Get the right habits to deal with either depression or obesity and you will likely manage the other much more effectively. True that you can only see obesity on a person, but I would argue that when you get rid of your obesity, you will also feel much better in your mind and confidence.

A new study at the University of Alabama at Birmingham (UAB) confirms the relationship between depression and abdominal obesity.

"We found that in a sample of young adults during a 15-year period, those who started out reporting high levels of depression gained weight at a faster rate than others in the study, but starting out overweight did not lead to changes in depression," said UAB Assistant Professor of Sociology Belinda Needham, Ph.D.. The study appears in the June issue of the American Journal of Public Health. Our study is important because if you are interested in controlling obesity, and ultimately eliminating the risk of obesity-related diseases, then it makes sense to treat people's depression," said Needham, who teaches in the UAB Department of Sociology and Social Work. "It is another reason to take depression seriously and not to think about it just in terms of mental health, but to also think about the physical consequences of mental health problems."

"My own waist circumference was also near fifty inches before I began to practice Zehhu" I told Joseph. "After only ten months, my waist was thirty-one inches and I was definitely feeling a lot better in my mind as well. This study gives us scientific data for something which we have always felt to be true. How many times have you heard of the phrase "fat and depressed"? Now we know why, because the same stress hormone called cortisol connects them.

"There is another idea that might help you deal with depression and is related to the food you eat," I said to Joseph. "There is a growing body of research which points to a link between wheat and depression.[47]

"Oh no, not bread, I live on bread at least three times a day!" Exclaimed Joseph.

"I am as much of a bread addict as you are, but it was nut until I had not eaten any grains for close to ten months that I experienced major body transformation results. I did not have a nutrition or strength conditioning expert to guide me. My expertise is purely from my experience, after having struggled for most of my life to lose weight.

"I tried just about every diet on the market. Those ten months were a real learning experience for me and I want to share it with you and anyone else who needs to lose weight and is struggling with depression.

"This idea of a link between wheat and depression is mentioned in passing in Charles Poliquin's 'Top 10 Carb Intake Rules for Optimal Body Composition.'[48] This article details how a low-carb, high-protein diet is ideal, but there are rules to follow in order to get the maximum benefits. Here is a summary of his rules which are most applicable to us and others battling depression and fat:

"1. Completely eliminate wheat, as it can raise blood sugar levels just like sugar. Avoid white bread at all costs. If you do eat grains, eat barley or rye or oats. And try to get most of your carbs from fruits and vegetables.

---

47 http://hashimashi.com/cut-grains-lean/

48 By Charles Poliquin http://www.charlespoliquin.com/Blog/tabid/130/EntryId/600/Poliquins-Top-10-Carb-Intake-Rules-for-Optimal-Body-Composition.aspx

"Indeed, a review published in the European Journal of Clinical Nutrition points to the fact that vegetables and fruit are preferable to even low glycemic wheat and grain-based foods.[49]

"I did not start to experience getting leaner until I cut out breads, even whole wheat breads. Every day I used to have whole grain bread in the morning, whole wheat pita, whole wheat burrito, whole wheat all the time. My body never changed while eating breads, whether I was doing cardio, or not; whether I was lifting weights, or not. I could not see any changes.

"And in fact, my A1C test, which gets to a certain level when you are type 2 diabetic, was just about there. I was already on the path, on the cusp of diabetes. And after six months, that AC1 test fell to a normal level. You should get your A1C test Joseph, because research has shown that test to be a better predictor of health than cholesterol, body mass index or blood pressure.[50]

"2. You might be allergic to wheat which can lead to adrenal exhaustion that can result in fatigue, depression and insomnia.[51] Those are symptoms that I have grappled with for many years, especially depression and insomnia. I can say that for me, the removal of bread has

---

49 Benn, B., Green, T. Glycemic Index and Glycemic Load: Measurement Issues and their Effect on Diet-Disease Relationships. European Journal of Clinical Nutrition. December 2007. 61(Suppl 1), 122-131.

Nilsson, A., Ostman, E., Granfeldt, Y., Bjorck, I. Effect of Cereal Test Breakfasts Differing in Glycemic Index and Content of Indigestible Carbohydrates on Daylong Glucose Tolerance in Healthy Subjects. American Journal of Clinical Nutrition. March 2008. 87(3), 645-654.

50 Goode, K., John, J., Rigby, A., Kilpatrick, E., Atkin, S., Bragadeesh, T., Clark, A., Cleland, J. Elevated Glycated Hemoglobin is a Strong Predictor of Mortality in Patients with Left Ventricular Systolic Dysfunction who are not Receiving Treatment for Diabetes Mellitus. Heart. 2009. 95, 917-923.

51 Katz, A., Falchuk, Z., Strober, W., Shwachman, H. Gluten-Sensitive Enteropathy. Inhibition of Cortisol of the Effect of Gluten Protein in Vitro. New England Journal of Medicine. July 1976. 295(3), 131-135.

helped to deal with depression. I wish my doctors had prescribed grain removal ten years ago.'"

"3. Make your main carb intake consist of fibrous foods such as kale, broccoli spinach, onions, mushrooms, peppers, and cauliflower.[52]

"4. Eat dark colored fruits like blueberries, strawberries and raspberries because their high levels of antioxidants help get rid of free radicals that cause aging and inflammation.

"5. Dark colored berries also help to keep your sugar levels low and stable which is good for weight loss and a better mood. Make sure that you fully chew berries or other dark thin skinned fruit to receive their full benefits.[53]

"6. Replace grains with greens like lettuce and spinach, because greens will provide more antioxidants, vitamins, and minerals as opposed to grains, which are lower in micronutrients. In addition, phytates—the salts of phytic acid that are found in high content in whole grains— block the absorption of many minerals, especially zinc, iron, manganese, and calcium.[54]

"7. Even though fruits are great foods loaded with nutrients, they also contain fructose. Fructose in too high quantities can slow down

---

52 Wolever, T., Campbell, J., Geleva, D., Anderson, H. High-Fiber Cereal Reduces Postprandial Insulin Responses in Hyperinsulinemic but not Normoinsulinemic Subjects. Diabetes Care. June 2004. 27(6), 1281-1285.

53 Clegg, M., Pratt, M., Meade, C., Henry, C. The Addition of Raspberries and Blueberries to a Starch-Based Food Does not Alter the Glycaemic Response. British Journal of Nutrition. August 2011. 106, 335-338.

54 Brites, C., Trigo, M., Carrapico, B., Alvina, M., Bessa, R. Maize and Resistant Starch Enriched Breads Reduce Postprandial Glycemic Responses in Rats. Nutrition Research. April 2011. 31(4), 302-308.

Hayashi, K., Hara, H., Asvarujanon, P., Aoyama, Y., Luangpituksa, P. Ingestion of Insoluble Dietary Fibre Increased Zinc and Iron Absorption and Restored Growth Rate and Zinc Absorption Suppressed by Dietary Phytate in Rats. British Journal of Nutrition. October 2001. 86(4), 3443-451.

thyroid function, reducing metabolism and negatively affecting body composition.

"One study compared the effect of a diet high in fructose with one high in glucose. After ten weeks, the fructose group had significantly elevated levels of cholesterol and insulin, while insulin sensitivity and fat metabolism decreased. They also gained significantly more total fat and an even greater percentage of abdominal fat than the glucose group. Further research shows that this extra insulin causes dysfunction of cells, and in addition to the negative effect on body composition, it accelerates aging, vascular degeneration, and development of diabetes.[55]

"8. The best time to load up on carbs is the first ten minutes following your workout. Insulin sensitivity is at its highest after a workout making this the critical time to take in carbs like a potato, banana, oatmeal or kasha to maximize muscle mass gains.[56]

"9. Use supplements that promote insulin sensitivity with high-carb post-workout meals such as taurine, arginine, magnesium, and R-form alpha lipoic acid. Adding them to your post-workout meal will help send glucose to muscle cells instead of fat cells.

"10. Add protein to your post-workout carb meal. Protein is a critical part of post-workout nutrition because your muscles are primed for feeding and need amino acids for peak recovery. Essential amino acids

---

55 Bousova, I., Pruchova, Z., Trnkova, L., Drsata, J. Comparison of Glycation of Glutathione S-Transferase by Methylglyoxal, Glucose, or Fructose. Molecular and Cellular Biochemistry. May 2011. Published Ahead of Print.

Boaz, L., Moshe, W. Fructose Triggers DNA Modification and Damage in an Escherichia Coli Plasmid. Nutritional Biochemistry. April 2001. 12(4), 235-241.

Stanhope, K., Schwarz, J., Keim, N., Briffen, S., et al. Consuming Fructose-Sweetened, not Glucose-Sweetened Beverages Increases Visceral Adiposity and Lipids and Decreases Insulin Sensitivity in Overweight/Obese Humans. Journal of Clinical Investigation. May 2009. 119(5), 1322-1334.

56 Hopps, E., Caimi, G. Exercise in Obesity Management. Journal of Sports Medicine and Physical Fitness. June 2011. 51(2), 275-282.

(EAAs), particularly the branched-chain amino acids (BCAAs), have been shown to trigger protein synthesis and fat loss.[57]

There are several sports performance supplements on the market that build strength, repair muscle and reduce recovery time, both plant or whey based. This information will be more beneficial to you once you start weight training to build muscle. In the meantime, let's focus on cleaning up your diet and getting you moving.

"How can I ever give up bread?"

"Try it out for a week, even a day and see how you feel. If you can gain some relief from depression by managing the type of food you eat, isn't that worth it?

Out of desperation, I cut grains completely out of my diet. While sitting and noshing on my second blueberry muffin at midnight, after having had a full day of refined processed grains, egg sandwich in the morning, pizza in the afternoon, pasta late lunch and a hero at night, I was just totally beside myself because I knew that I was not hungry.

How could I be hungry? But if I was not hungry, why was I craving more at midnight? However, after only six months, I was 75 pounds lighter, looked dramatically different, and the effects on lifting my mood were palpable.

---

57 Sharp, C., Pearson, D. Amino Acid Supplements and Recovery from High-Intensity Resistance Training. Journal of Strength and Conditioning Research. 2010. 24(4), 1125-1130.

Qin, L., Xun, P., Bujnowski, D., Daviglus, M., Van Horn, L., Stamler, J., He, K. Higher Branched-Chain amino Acid Intake is Associated with a Lower Prevalence of Being Overweight or Obese in Middle-Aged East Asian and Western Adults. The Journal of Nutrition. 2010. 141(2), 249-254.

Kerksick, C., Harvey, T., Stout, J., Campbell, B., Wilborn, C., Kreider, R., Kalman, D., Ziegenfuss, T., Lopez, H., Landis, J., Ivy, J., Antonio, J. International Society of Sports Nutrition position stand: nutrient timing. Journal of the International Society of Sports Nutrition. 2008. 3, 5-17. http://www.jissn.com/content/5/1/17#B85

You might want to check out a similar approach of real food, little to no highly refined processed grains, lifting your body off the couch to do pushups, walk, run, swim, lift weights to lift yourself out of your depression![58]

"This is getting depressing."

"What?"

"Bread is my favorite food. Cold, hot, muffins, pancakes, anything made from flour, cookies, hot rolls, hot bread and bagels. How will I ever survive without bread?"

"Well, maybe this is something for you to try out. Maybe the wheat, the gluten is something that you are sensitive to. It is worth taking a week off from wheat if you can get your sanity back."

"I don't know. I cannot imagine."

"Well, I am not going to feel sorry for you. If you go wheat free and get your life back.

"Refined wheat bread free affects everything from my depression to my weight, from my anxiety to complexion, from being negative to feeling optimistic, from living with heartburn to none, and anyone who deals with heartburn knows what a relief that is, to have none! Recently I chalked it off to just my own natural predisposition, somehow genetically. I just cannot tolerate highly refined processed wheat bread, but why would anyone else speak much about it. To my pleasant surprise, I found quite a few experts answering the question for you in their own way with their own points of view.

"First off, without knowing the chemical reasons or the nutritional science behind it, I will answer from my own experience. Is refined wheat bread so bad for you that you have to X it out of your life?

---

58 http://hashimashi.com/is-gluten-making-you-depressed/

Why Highly Refined Processed Wheat Bread
Is bad for You Based on Anecdotal Evidence

"I am neither a nutritionist nor a doctor. However, I am a longtime sufferer of depression, obesity, and anxiety and in only ten months I went from 250 to 175 pounds, from a 48" waist to a 32" waist, from a really depressed negative paranoid and anxious individual to much more confident, optimistic and even-keeled. It is possible that what I did does not prove that wheat is bad for you. It could be because I went on a high vegetable diet.

"When I stopped eating wheat, I had to eat something in its place, and since I did not savor the idea of eating lamb chops all day, my method was to eat vegetables wherever I would normally eat bread. If in the morning I would have an egg sandwich on whole wheat bread or whole wheat bagel; instead of the bread, I loaded up on vegetables and made an egg omelet with tons of vegetables, onion, garlic, broccoli, spinach, mushrooms and red pepper, sautéed in olive oil.

"In only one day, my heartburn was gone! How often did I suffer from heartburn? Every day."

"I carry Tums with me all the time. I have terrible heartburn just about every day. I have to try this out."

"I know for a fact that it was the wheat that was bad for me, or was it the lack of vegetables? The reason I believe it was the wheat is that many times I tried to have sandwiches that had tons of vegetables. I just did not want to stop eating bread no matter what. I kicked and screamed that I must have bread, even three times a day, at least once, I needed my bread fix to feel full. That was my rationale. Is wheat bad for you? I cannot say for sure, but have you experienced any of the following symptoms after eating wheat-based meals like bread, pasta, cereal or pizza:

1. Heartburn

For years, I lived with heartburn and Rolaids to get some relief. I had no idea how dangerous heartburn is for the esophagus. I can only hope that I have stopped having the heartburn in time from eating away from the healthy cells. Every day, within an hour or so of my wheat meal, boom, and my insides were on fire. Fire!

"Not only do you lose your desire for living, you even lose the desire for moving! I just wanted to stay put and not go anywhere. Forget about exercise, I did not even want to go for a walk."

Joseph said, "You have been trying to get me outside to go for a walk for months. I did not even think that maybe the heartburn I have all day is a factor, if not the factor for my not wanting to go no matter how much you have encouraged me to do so."

"Well, of course," I said to him, "if you have heartburn the way I used to, I can totally understand why you don't want to go anywhere, even for a simple walk. I would answer the question is refined wheat bread bad for you—you bet. Is it worth eating wheat? Never. Do I love the thought of fresh-baked warm bread? Yes, but the thought of fiery heartburn is even worse and I prefer to avoid the pain and drop the bread. Try dropping the wheat for a few days and see if your heartburn goes away and if it does, perhaps then you will feel good enough to go for a walk."

"How can wheat be bad for you when in ancient times, people spoke of eating bread in the morning and man does not live by bread alone? Clearly, people lived on bread!"

"As you will see in some other additional data I have mentioned below, there are people who say that if we were eating the wheat of our ancestors, we would not be suffering like we do today. The wheat produced today is hybridized and our genetics have no way of dealing with it, other than to protest by having our bodies react in negative ways."

2. Bloating and floating away like a balloon!

"Have you ever been fat? Are you still fat? How many diets have you tried out? Have you ever experienced getting bloated? Especially after highly processed meals that contain bread, pasta, pizza, flour products?

"I can only speak for myself, but just from the bloating point of view, without wheat, my face even changed after a good six months, from the previous blown up cheeks and double chin to a much leaner version of me and without hours and hours of exercise."

Is wheat bad for you? I am quite sure that it is terrible. Today's modern version of wheat is a disaster.

"Before wheat, my entire body was a bowl of jello. Believe me; I was invisible on the street, meaning nobody had much interest in saying hello to me or even responding to my greetings."

"I can relate to that. I have felt invisible as if I do not exist or ever existed for years. The only way I know I exist is when I see myself in the mirror, which is about it."

"Suddenly, after six months, I became visible. I became worthy of a hello. I went from Jello to Hello! So, in terms of bloating, being invisible, face turning to jello, is wheat bad for you? Yes, no question!

3. Weight Loss

"I have one word for that four letter word 'diet'—impossible! I had a closet full of diet books. I have been on a diet since I was a baby, starting off with Weight Watchers pizza and every other possible variation of diet in between, from fruitarian to vegan to macrobiotic. Nothing helped the heartburn, bloating, discomfort, and the weight just kept going up and up like a balloon. Why is it that when I stopped eating refined wheat bread, the weight started to melt off almost effortlessly? You think I do not know the frustration of being forever fat?

"I know you have been struggling with losing weight for many years. If I can tell you just one tip, STOP EATING refined wheat bread! My theory is that we all have different physiology and just because you see slim people wolfing down pizza and staying slim, that does not mean that you can do the same! For whatever reason, your body just might not be able to tolerate wheat in any of its forms. Try it out for one month. Give it thirty days. Count day one and keep going. Tell me what happens after you have gone for thirty days without wheat; no bread, pasta and grains. Just make sure that you are eating vegetables. It is possible that you are just one of the people for whom wheat is not only bad, but is also toxic and keeps your body inflamed and fat for as long as you keep eating it. If you have been trying to lose weight for too many years, the answer to the question is, wheat is bad for you!

4. Fat Loss

Some people just think about losing weight all the time, but ideally, I think we all know that we want to lose fat. We want to be more muscular. I can tell you that outside of when I was a teen, I had not been able to see any muscles for many years.

5. Wearing Clothes that FIT!

Are you tired of walking around in big sweaters? Are you tired of walking around in oversized shirts? That is pretty much all I wore for a long time because it was large enough to cover the big bulging belly that I have not yet shown you a picture of. It is just too embarrassing! Do you want to be able to walk into a clothing store and pretty much buy an item off the rack and be able to wear it comfortably? No struggle to lose weight, get on your pants, or fit in your clothes and feel like a human being? Wheat is bad for you if you want to fit in your clothes.

6. Depression and Anxiety

I have recently found more information demonstrating that wheat might be culpable for depression scientifically, but I can tell you from my own experience that it appears to be a factor. Before going on antidepressants, you should try going off refined wheat bread! As soon as I stopped wheat, I started to calm down. It takes time, but it is easier to manage depression more effectively when you are feeling better physically.

That is my anecdotal evidence that eliminating wheat can yield transformative results for both your mind and body.

"I want you to read one more article so an expert can weigh in. It's called 'Why You Should STOP Eating Whole Wheat Bread' and it's written by a certified nutrition specialist named Mike Geary. In it he talks about what wheat and gluten actually do to your insides and how eating it can cause heart disease, diabetes, and even cancer. He even talks about just how much your blood sugar spikes after eating specific foods. You'll be shocked.

"Clearly, if you asked Mike Geary if wheat is bad for you, he would say: Stop Eating Wheat and Start to Heal from the inside out! The important takeaway then is that for you to have the best fighting chance against depression, you must eat the healthiest food possible for your body and mind. Eating real food will give you a fighting chance to beat depression, because eating real food along with the core body workouts of squats, deadlifts, walking/running, and pushups is going to transform your body from fat to fit. When your body starts to transform from out of shape to in shape, it is going to have a big impact on how you see yourself as well as how your mind will perceive life.

"After six months of eating real food and doing the core workouts that I have suggested, do not be surprised if you are 75 pounds lighter, or you have trimmed down to a 32-inch waist or you have lowered your cholesterol by over 100 points. I was surprised when that happened to me. But now that I am telling you what is possible from eating real food and moving your body more, you do not have to be surprised because these results can and will happen if you are consistent.

"I have spent a lot of time in this lesson of 'watering the vineyard' because simply changing the type of food that you eat can effect an amazing mind and body transformation. You just have to give it a shot. Give yourself one month. Eat real food, lots of vegetables, organic lean proteins, some nuts and seeds, snack on fruits when you want something sweet, drink water, and watch how your body will change like magic.

"Even more important will be the gradual change in your attitude. You have your best fighting chance to beat depression when you feel healthy in your body. Next time you check yourself in the mirror to see if you exist, let us hope that you like the newer version of yourself that you will see."

"There is no way that I will be able to have no wheat, no bread. Why does it have to be so extreme?"

"I have a suggestion for you. This is a very simple type of meal plan that I have used for myself. Instead of completely eliminating bread, try the following on for size: Make sure you have breakfast every day. The more you ensure that you get a good breakfast in; the less likely it will be that you eat in the evening. Since you are going to make sure to have a good breakfast, try to do your walk or any other workout in the morning after you wake up. The benefit here of working out in the morning is that breakfast will then be a much better time to have your slices of bread. Since you have been overdosing on bread for so long, I recommend you limit yourself to a couple of slices in the morning and a couple for lunch with no more bread or heavy carbs after two or three p.m. After a workout, your muscles will be much more receptive to the faster digesting carbs which you get from your bread.

"I also think that if you can, go for whole grain rye bread or a sprouted bread like Ezekiel. So for example, after your workout, lightly grill a couple of slices of whole grain rye or spelt or stone ground whole wheat with a teaspoon of extra virgin olive oil. Cut up a bunch of vegetables, a couple slices of tomato, onion, a handful of spinach.

"In another pan, put in another teaspoon of extra virgin olive oil, sauté some garlic cloves and mushrooms, add a few egg whites or if your doctor agrees a whole egg as well. When the omelet is set, take out your grilled bread from the first pan, put the raw vegetables on top of your bread, add the omelet, a tablespoon of shredded parmesan, and voila, you have a very filling breakfast that should easily keep you going for a few hours. Another easy breakfast is a bowl of oatmeal with banana and a teaspoon of honey.

If you do not feel like cooking, as you have mentioned many times, try this out:

1/2 cup of dry oats
1/4 cup of grapenuts
tablespoon of raisins
tablespoon of walnuts
One banana sliced
One orange or grapefruit
handful of grapes
Cup of almond or hemp milk

That is about as easy a breakfast as you can get. When you get hungry again, have a fruit, plain yogurt, or some nuts.

"Do the same type of sandwich for lunch. Grill your bread, add raw vegetables, add a protein like tofu, veggie burger, turkey, or tuna, add some pickles and olives and maybe a slice of swiss, add some avocado. This is another easy to prepare lunch that you can have at home or take with you on the way.

"For a snack, when you have a little time, you can put a plain yogurt in a bowl, add some fruit, top with walnuts and a drizzle of honey and that will definitely satisfy some of your cravings for ice cream.

"By dinner time you would have had four meals, so I am pretty confident that you will not be famished. The big benefit of having already eaten four meals is that you are nourishing your body throughout the day. You have already had your bread fix, raw vegetables, some fruit, some nuts, and probiotic yogurt.

"At dinner, you will not need to have bread or pasta. Focus on having a dinner like chickpeas and veggie burger or sweet potato and salmon or brown rice and tofu. I suggest that you finish having dinner by seven o'clock so you can easily get to sleep by ten. That will give you a full eight hours by six in the morning and you can start your day all over again. I guarantee you that if you follow such a program for three months, you are going to be turning into a new man. Go it over with your doctor or nutritionist and give it a shot. What do you have to lose besides your weight and depression?"

"Okay, that sounded a lot more doable than the absolute no wheat lecture that you just gave me."

"Remember, when I say no wheat, I am speaking about no highly refined and processed wheat breads. There are plenty of nourishing whole grains like quinoa, millet, spelt, brown rice and grain like fruits like buckwheat that are healthy and have been used by many civilizations throughout history. These are just some ideas for how you can start to rebuild your mind and body one day at a time. Before you know it, you will be rebuilding your life. I believe you can rebuild your life, but you do need a fighting chance and by feeding yourself the best foods that you can, especially raw vegetables and fruit and nuts, all of these nutrients that you have barely had for the last ten years, they are going to help your energy levels, help you to exercise and get stronger, and help you to think better thoughts."

"I would do the no wheat if I thought it was sustainable. I just wanted to see if there is another option and I think you gave me one that sounds pretty simple for even a divorced man like me in a three-hundred-square-foot studio with a hot plate for a stove. I would appreciate more recipes and workouts as well, for lower body workouts and upper body workouts and the affirmations that you speak about too. Just make them easy enough for a single guy like me to understand and do without too much trouble. I hate to cook and I hate to clean." No worries Joseph, I will give you more advanced workouts once you have lost the weight.

Lessons of the Vineyard

PROTECTING THE VINEYARD

During the growing process, it is necessary to adjust for bad weather. In the case of the vineyard, the viticulturist has to ensure that the temperature stays constant and moderate for the vineyard so that the grapes do not wither if the weather becomes too hot or too cold. Similarly, we cannot assume that we are not going to hit bad weather along the way. For someone who has been living in depression, you have already come across significant turbulence, enough to push you deep into the pit of depression.

If and when we are starting to be successful in moving beyond the depression, when we are just starting to blossom, it is more than likely that here and there we are going to hit a cold spell. Maybe someone will not be so friendly to us, maybe we are still feeling the effects of an estrangement from a friend or family member, or perhaps the weather will be too hot. We might not think we can sustain the effort necessary to keep moving forward and we are in jeopardy of burning out.

For all these cases, the same applies to us as the owner of the vineyard will do for his grape clusters that are just starting to mature. Stay the course. Keep the temperature stable. For us this means to not let the waves that we encounter on our journey derail us from making progress. Just as the field owner will protect his vineyard, so too we must protect ourselves. We do this by taking the actions necessary to keep moving forward, shield ourselves from excessive drama, and stay the course on the path to freedom from living in the room of depression despite the inevitable setbacks and curve balls that every person can face in life.

In other words, don't give up!

LESSONS OF THE VINEYARD

HARVESTING THE VINEYARD

At long last, the grapes are reaching maturity and it is time to start harvesting the grapes.

The time for the vineyard to grow is a known amount, approximately six months after the seeds have been planted, and you are going to have a field full of glistening clusters of grapes on your trestles. The way we apply this to our own lives is by creating goals.

Now the goals I am speaking about here is not a to-do list or a shopping list. I am thinking more along the lines of how the vineyard grows. There is only one thing the vineyard is going to do, and that is to grow grapes, nothing else; no oranges, tomatoes, cucumbers, nothing but grapes.

There is a great lesson there for us, that when anyone is trying to achieve a goal, and certainly a person who is pulling themselves out of depression, the best way to do it is to stay very focused, like a laser beam, on their objective. Just as a vineyard only produces grapes, I believe that the message here for us is to do the same. Be focused on a specific goal and do not get distracted by attempting to grow berries from the same vineyard. In the plant world that can never happen, but in our world, we can distract ourselves all day and night with a myriad of things to be busy with. The goals can all be singular and straightforward. For example, go to sleep by 10 p.m. and wake up at 6 a.m. Eat a healthy breakfast, either fresh fruit or freshly squeezed vegetable juice, a vegetable egg omelet with a lot of vegetables such as onion, garlic, mushroom, spinach and tomato. Get to work on time. Focus on doing a great job whatever it is that you do.

Set aside time to work out, to access the transformation that you can have for your body and mind from the powerful exercises to fight depression that we have discussed. Even if you just start with one goal like doing deadlifts or going to sleep earlier, you are going to see a benefit and eventually a big change.

Meeting these goals is going to motivate you to make another goal, which will become a habit. Good habits are going to help you meet your goals and each time that you do, you will be inspired to keep going. Start small. There is no reason to make outlandish goals you do not believe you could ever do, like walking across the Grand Canyon on a tightrope. Your goal is to cross the bridge from living in the state of depression to a state of moving beyond your depression and living.

Why moving beyond and not curing? I am not sure that depression can be cured. If it is within the person genetically and/or chemically, then for sure it cannot be cured. If it is a consequence of external events that have built up like waves until you are drowning, then those painful memories will always be with you. While I believe that obesity can be cured, I am of the opinion that depression cannot. If it cannot, then what can we do? The answer is we can leave the room of depression. We can stop living in the depression and start to move beyond that place. This is the whole focus here, to stop the descent and to start moving forward toward a new life. Once you are not living in depression, then you start moving toward living in the new rooms, the new visualizations that you have been creating for yourself.

The source of your depression might always be there, but as long as you are not living in that room of depression, as long as you are not living in that space, then you can cross the bridge from depression to life. You will cross the bridge from the state of depression to a state of living the best life possible that you can create now. When you have begun the process of creating goals to move toward, you will be tempted to keep revisiting the memories of the past.

Just as the viticulturist will not keep going back during the harvest to pick up fallen grapes, so too it is best not to look back, to accept that what has happened in the past has already occurred and that cannot be changed. Instead, keep moving forward toward picking out the finest grapes and creating the best wine to enjoy with your family and friends.

LESSONS OF THE VINEYARD

SELECTING THE BEST GRAPES

The process of winnowing when it comes to crops is the separation of the chaff from the wheat. The process as it applies to grapes has multiple steps. There is the initial separation of the grape from the stalk. Once the grapes are separated from the stalk, they are pressed and then after a certain amount of time, there might be an addition of yeast and/or sugar to the mix. Once the primary fermentation is completed, there is another filtering out of the liquid from the grapes, which then will sit usually for at least five to six months depending on the amount of alcohol desired. As you know, some wines can be kept in their containers for decades and you will pay top dollar to acquire it.

In the case of separating wheat, the choice is easily made after the harvest. The farmer will cast the collected wheat into the air and the wind will blow away the chaff, leaving only the wheat kernels. At least that is how it was done in ancient times. In the case of grapes, the grapes must be separated from the stalk before additional processing can take place. What actionable lessons can we learn from nature here?

Selecting the best grapes from the stalk is analogous to focusing on the best parts of your life. The room of depression will always exist in your home, but hopefully by the end of reading this book, you will relegate that room to the basement and lock the door. Now we are learning that we have to focus on the best rooms, objectives, goals, no matter how simple they might seem to someone else. It is critical that a person who has lived so deeply in depression celebrate every win, no matter how small. We do this by focusing on what we have and not on what we don't have.

I know that is a huge challenge for a person who is used to living in the room of depression, but it is worth taking on and whatever you can find in your life that is working, that looks like the glistening best grape clusters, keep them in your mind and gaze on them and get rid of the stalks and damaged berries.

Stop revisiting the painful memories of the past. Stop focusing on the worst of your life and move toward creating a better future. This is also a good time to have gratitude for the good grapes that we yielded from the harvest. Harvesting a ton of grapes will do us no good if they are all rotten. Harvesting a ton of grapes when 80% of them can be used for making wine is something to be happy about.

Without gratitude for what we do have, how can we ever move forward? We will be stuck in our moaning over everything that has gone wrong in our lives and we will lose sight of the fact that we do have some good grapes to make wine. Having gratitude is probably one of the most difficult habits for a person who has lived in depression. I believe that a common feature of being in depression has its roots in a sense of arrogance.

"How can you say that!" Joseph exclaimed when I said just that to him. "I am not arrogant. I might be broken-hearted, I might be abandoned, I might be without my family and career, but how can you ever think that I or anyone else in depression is arrogant? I am offended."

"I have no intention of offending you. Think about the definition of arrogance: an offensive display of superiority or self-importance; overbearing pride.[59] I know all the tragedies of your life and sympathize and even empathize. However, you are not the only one in the world who has experienced such setbacks. Your parents suffered unspeakable crimes in the concentration camps, but you are not the only one on earth whose parents suffered war crimes. And even if you had been in

---

59 http://dictionary.reference.com/browse/arrogance

the camps, you were not the only one. There were millions of others throughout history. It is a great shame and despicable fact that there are cultures and/or countries that believe that they have the right to destroy others and they have the free will to act on their bloodthirsty fantasies of ruling the world and ridding the world of their enemies.

"By the same token, you have the right and the choice to not destroy yourself. It is not enough that the Nazis murdered your family and scarred your mother for life, physically and mentally; why do you have to use this memory to destroy your own life? In addition, if there were six million Jewish people that were murdered, that means there are millions of survivors. Practically every Jewish family on earth was affected, so you are not the only one who had to deal with being the relative of a survivor. The number of civilians killed totaled from 38 to 55 million, including 19 to 25 million from war-related disease and famine. This means that besides the genocide of the Jewish people, there were between 32 and 49 million other people slaughtered, some because they were Roma, homosexuals, handicapped, or Slavs.

"The total military dead were from 22 to 25 million including deaths in captivity of about five million prisoners of war.[60] So instead of being grateful that you did not have to live through such a horror, you have allowed the horror of what happened to affect your life to the point that you became non-functional. So when I say that it is arrogance, it is as if you think that war can happen to others but that you are above everyone else. I know you do not believe you are superior in that way, but I want to point out to you that many millions of people have mourned over their relatives that were taken from them.

"You are not the only one and if you think of the definition of humble, that is what makes you human. You are human like everyone else, and we are all subject to tragedies such as these. All of us have to be modest in our own view of our self-importance. Of course we have to

---

60 http://en.wikipedia.org/wiki/World_War_II_casualties

mourn, but we cannot destroy ourselves in the process. Does that make sense to you?"

"I never thought of it that way."

"The same holds true for the other waves of depression that you have spoken about which were traumatic for you. For example, what you told me about the drowning where you saved the tourist. Look at some of the key facts about drowning: Drowning is the third leading cause of unintentional injury death worldwide, accounting for 7% of all injury-related deaths. There are an estimated 372,000 annual drowning deaths worldwide. Global estimates may significantly underestimate the actual public health problem related to drowning.

"Children, males, and individuals with increased access to water are most at risk of drowning.[61] In your story, the person who drowned was a complete stranger and you did not drown as a result of saving him. You were safe and he was safe. It was a traumatic experience because you believed that you were going to die, but in the end, not only did you live, but you were able to save a person, a son, a father and a husband. Why not look at that in a positive way? You actually saved another human being and you were still alive. You did not have to sacrifice your life to save his and you are still safe to this very day."

"It is true. I just focus on the trauma of that moment and not on the outcome, which was good for all of us. He lived, his kids and wife and parents had their father, husband, and son, and I had done a good deed."

"Then you had the situation where your dad was killed in a car crash when you were a young man. Do you have any idea how many people are affected by car-related accidents and fatalities?"

"No, I do not."

"Take a look at this from the Annual Global Road Crash Statistics: Nearly 1.3 million people die in road crashes each year, on average 3,287 deaths a day. An additional 20 to 50 million are injured or disabled.

---

61 http://www.who.int/mediacentre/factsheets/fs347/en/

More than half of all road traffic deaths occur among young adults ages 15-44. Road traffic crashes rank as the ninth leading cause of death and account for 2.2% of all deaths globally. Road crashes are the leading cause of death among young people ages 15 to 29, and the second leading cause of death worldwide among young people ages 5 to 14. Each year nearly 400,000 people under 25 die on the world's roads, on average over 1,000 a day.

"Over 90% of all road fatalities occur in low- and middle-income countries, which have less than half of the world's vehicles. Road crashes cost USD $518 billion globally, costing individual countries from 1 to 2% of their annual GDP. Road crashes cost low- and middle-income countries USD $65 billion annually, exceeding the total amount received in developmental assistance. Unless action is taken, road traffic injuries are predicted to become the fifth leading cause of death by 2030.

In the report of Annual United States Road Crash Statistics: Over 37,000 people die in road crashes each year. An additional 2.35 million are injured or disabled and over 1,600 children under 15 years of age die each year. Nearly 8,000 people are killed in crashes involving drivers ages 16 to 20. Road crashes cost the United States $230.6 billion per year, or an average of $820 per person. Road crashes are the single greatest annual cause of death of healthy U.S. citizens traveling abroad.[62]

"These are sobering statistics to say the least. They do not minimize the pain that you felt from losing your father at a young age, but they might give you a better perspective in terms of how you react to such a tragedy.

"Unfortunately, none of us are immune and all that I want for you is that you have the opportunity to live your best life possible, despite the challenges that you have faced.

---

62 http://asirt.org/Initiatives/Informing-Road-Users/Road-Safety-Facts/ Road-Crash-Statistics

"In order to do that, I think it could be helpful for all of us to always work on being humble, accept that we are all human, we are all vulnerable and that can motivate us to be grateful for everything that we have now and help us to focus on the good of our lives and not the most negative part.

In this case of your dad, imagine if your mother had been in the car. I am sorry that you experienced this loss of your father, but I am also confident that if your father could speak to you today, I believe he would tell you to live every day in the best way possible and he would never want his accident to be a source or a cause for you to give up on life. Does that make sense?"

"Yes, it does. I think I know where you are going. Next you are going to tell me that I am not the only one who has been a victim to crime, robbery, and assault."

"Sadly, that is true. Since 1975 there have been over a million violent crimes a year in the United States alone. That does not include property crime and a whole list of assorted other assaults on innocent people. I know it is difficult to recover from such a trauma but I hope that you will give yourself the permission to break free from the prison that you have been in. The criminals who assaulted you are the ones who belong in prison, not you!"

"Yes, why have I been the one in prison? For over ten years now my apartment here has been similar to a jail and I have been the defendant, the judge, the inmate, and the guard. But what about estrangement, that is probably not too common?"

"There are no accurate or authoritative statistics on parental alienation or family estrangements that I know about. The one fact that we do know is that in America, there is one divorce approximately every 36 seconds. That's nearly 2,400 divorces per day, 16,800 divorces per week and 876,000 divorces a year.

"A twelve-year study commissioned by the Family Law Section of the American Bar Association of over 1,000 divorces found that 'parental alienation,' the programming of a child against the other parent, occurs regularly, sixty percent (60%) of the time, and sporadically another 20%.[63] According to this astronomical number, of the 876,000 divorces a year, we can expect that over 500,000 of these divorces will result in the regular programming of a child against the target parent."

"Let us look at a few of the known methods of alienation which alienating parents employ to program their children away from the target parent. Many of them are apparent. Others, though insidious, are just as pernicious. Some methods are intentional, deliberate, and willful, while others might even be utilized subconsciously by the alienating parent. One of the 'basic techniques' alienating parents use is to send the message, either overtly or subtly, that the target parent is insignificant or irrelevant to the child.[64] This may be done by ignoring the target parent at social functions and elsewhere, or by denying or refusing to acknowledge his existence.[65]

"Another way is by choosing to never talk about the other parent. A subtle message is sent that the other parent is insignificant.[66] The target parent's insignificance can also be signaled by using body language to show that he is unworthy or insignificant.[67] The alienating parent might avoid eye contact with the target, use a hand gesture that is dismissive or indicates negativity, look away when he is present, or, when the child raises

---

63 http://www.thebrooklyndivorcelawyers.com/publications/Father%20What%20 Father%20-%20NYSBA%20FLR%20(Part%20I).pdf

64 See Clawar & Rivlin, Id., Ch. VII, (The Female Factor: Why Women Programme More Than Men)Although alienation might be employed by either parent, because it is more likely to be employed by mothers than by fathers, and because mothers are more likely to obtain custody than fathers (see Brandes, 4 Law and the Family New York §§ 1:2 and 1:3), for ease of reading the story about Joseph, the target parent is referred to in the masculine.

65 Clawar &Rivlin at 15 Id.

66 Ibid.

67 Clawar &Rivlin at 16, Id.

the other parent in conversation, abruptly terminate the conversation.[68] Children are attuned to these subtle signals and interestingly enough, often adopt them and 'mirror [these] physical pattern[s].'"

"You just gave me chills. The main feeling I have had over the last decade is that I never existed. I was just surgically removed from my own life, and I imagine I do not have to tell you how humiliating that feels."

"No, unfortunately you do not."

"I have experienced all of the methods that you cited which have always made me feel less than human, the sense that I have no significance as a man or as a father, I have witnessed the body language and I have been told by others how the mere mention of my name would abruptly terminate any conversation about me.

Just thinking about it crushes my heart. I feel so degraded and realize how I have had effectively no life with my children for over a decade. I go through a kaleidoscope of emotions from hopelessness to rage, utter humiliation to indignation and feel frozen that there is no point left in life.

"Between the courts forcing me out of my own home and the parental alienation that you describe, what hope can I have for any type of decent future? I do not want a future without my children."

"I am sure that your children do not want a future without you. The same way you are in pain, think of the anguish your children are feeling. It cannot be easy on them. You are only thinking of yourself. Do you think that your children wanted to lose their father? Do you think that your children want to know or hear or see that their father is depressed? Don't you think your children want to be proud of their father and see him as their protector? Imagine what it is like for a youngster or teenager to suddenly have to deal with the court order that forces you out of your home. The same court order is forcing you out of their home and lives.

---

68 Ibid.

"Do not believe that this is easy on them. If you keep going back to the narrative that you are the only one who has suffered here, I do not think that you can ever heal. You have to leave it alone, you have to let go. When you have a wound, you cover it with a Band-Aid® and stop touching it. Stop bringing up the past. We have been speaking for years now, and no matter how much we talk about them, we cannot change them, we can only change us, so how about just focusing on you?"

"Isn't that selfish to just focus on me? Isn't that the height of 'arrogance' to only think of myself?"

"I know you have been working on yourself. I have seen a lot of physical changes. I just think if you can really practice to let it go by focusing on everything that you need to be a healthier you, there is a much better chance of things changing in the future. At the minimum, you will become the best version of you, so if your children come back to you, they will find a healthier and happier father and I am confident that is what they want deep down inside. It is not selfish for you to focus on yourself. If you don't, who will? Only you can control what you think in your mind, what you say to yourself and others and what actions you take. You are the one, the only one, who has that control. So focusing on you is not selfish. It is taking responsibility for yourself. It is stopping the blame game and looking at others and their fields. Focusing on you is becoming more humble and looking at how you can improve your own field without constantly comparing yourself to others; their lives, their fields."

"You are right. From all my years of depression, I can say with absolute certainty that I cannot think of one way this depression has helped change anyone or anything outside of myself. For me, depression has just kept me in my state of misery. When I think of what depression has accomplished in my life, I have to admit, absolutely nothing. I am going to review everything we have spoken about and will really try to get my head screwed on straighter and focus on me only."

LESSONS OF THE VINEYARD

PRESSING THE WINE

"We are getting closer to the main event, living a good life with ourselves, family, and friends. We need one more step before the wine will be bottled and end up on our dinner table. The wine has to be pressed out of the grapes, and then the fermentation of the wine must take place. Pressure does not always result in a negative. Sometimes when we are feeling pressure, we assume that it cannot be for good, but in fact, just as pressure can create a diamond, so too can pressure create a better person, characteristics, and personality. In every situation in life, we are faced with opportunities to make choices. The decisions can be as simple as what to eat for breakfast or when you should tell your significant other that you are a late for boarding a plane.

"If your breakfast choices every day are a couple of donuts, a blueberry muffin, and french toast, you are clearly making a decision to keep getting fatter and out of shape. If you are working out ten hours a day, perhaps you will not be affected, but more likely than not, you barely work out right now and are lucky if you have enough time to get in 15 to 30 minutes for a walk or the treadmill. If you neglected to tell your wife, husband, or significant other that you are in line at the airport to get some food for the flight and they start to panic since the plane is boarding, even if it was not intentional, you still made a poor decision that fails to keep everyone safe that you care about in your life. You have to keep yourself safe by eating nutritious food and saving your cakes and partying for real celebrations like birthdays, weddings, anniversaries, and graduations. You must keep the ones you love safe by protecting them from negative thoughts about your safety as much as possible.

"You could say that this is all too much pressure for you, and you cannot handle the pressure of making better food choices, or you just cannot handle the pressure of being more aware of time and the sensitivities and reasonable fears of the most important person in your life who cares about your safety, but if you do say that this is too much pressure you are missing out on a great opportunity to become a better person. When you make wise lifestyle choices, you will reap the rewards in how you look and feel and keeping yourself in the best health possible.

"When you make wise choices regarding the sensitivities of the people you love and who love you, your relationships will be stronger because you will take actions that make you feel comfortable, confident, and secure. Keep your cell phone on and stay in touch with those who care about you. Try not to get lost in an airport while your plane is boarding. I speak from personal experience and I learned my lesson. That is the first lesson we can get from the pressing of the grapes. Pressure is good; pressure can transform a grape into wine, coal into diamonds, a person with poor lazy habits into a fine gentleman or woman; a great athlete, doctor, or financial analyst; a better father, mother, son or daughter.

"Let go of your fear of pressure or of your annoyance of pressure. Accept that it is in your best interest to keep improving all your life. Not a day will go by in your life that you cannot find an area to improve and that is okay. No one is perfect and there will always be challenges along the way. You will continue to be squeezed for the rest of your life to be better and you can accept every pressing for what it really is, an opportunity to grow in strength and character.

"The pressing of the grapes is also symbolic of squeezing out every morsel of good that you can from whatever it is that you have and wherever you are in your life at the moment. In order to do that, you really have to stay focused on the present. It is very easy to fall back into the habit of reviewing everything that went wrong in your life from a half hour ago to a half century ago, but what is the value there unless you learn specific lessons on what works and what does not work in life? Usually when people start looking back, they are not always happy with the view. Instead of looking back, think of your life now in the present and how you can improve your now and your future. Staying in the present and taking all the actions that you can to keep building a stronger life in all ways is a sure path to a much greater satisfaction in life.

When you focus on finding and squeezing out every drop of bad in your life, then you will always feel bad. When you are feeling bad, there is a good chance that you will not have much motivation to do anything that is very productive. Feeling bad is not the way to fire you up and get motivated to take action. Without action, nothing will get accomplished from all of the dreams you have in your life. You always wanted to be a writer? Well then, start writing. Who is stopping you? You do not have the time? How about watching an hour or two less of television every day and using that time to write? You always wanted to be an artist, programmer, musician, or doctor, what are you waiting for? Every moment that you mourn over the past, you are losing your present and your future. Make a commitment to find the one thing that you want to focus on in your life for this month, this quarter or this year. When you find that passion, you will make time for the actions that you must take in order to realize your dreams.

"Make the commitment to set aside time every day, whether an hour or ten hours. This is how you squeeze the wine from the grapes. One more lesson that I would like to draw from the pressing of the grapes is that we have to deal with the type of grapes that we harvested. We have to do our best to flavor our life as best as we can with the grapes that grew in our vineyard. Our vineyard as it stands right now is what our lives are in the present moment. It might be barren, it might be full. It might be a new field when you are a teen or in your twenties or it might be a field that is mature if you are in your forties and above. You might be at the beginning, middle, or end of your career or looking for a new one. You might be at the beginning of a new diet that you hope will help you shed the ten, twenty, fifty, or seventy-five pounds that will make you a healthier person in both body and mind.

"Cabernet grapes produce cabernet as merlot grapes produce merlot. Every type of wine is produced according to the type of grapes that were planted and the soil of the field. We are similar in that our lives reflect the seeds that we planted in our own field. Plant a lot of Ring-Dings and you will surely be overweight. Plant a lot of vegetables and real food and you will look awesome. Plant a lot of love and affection for yourself and the well-wishers in your life and you will see that same care reflected back to you. Plant a lot of action and you will see the results. Plant a lot of moping, sulking, marinating in the room of depression and you will see a lot of depression for yourself and many people fleeing your side to save themselves from your sadness.

"You can start today to build the life that you want tomorrow.

"Tomorrow might not happen the next day, but it will happen, a month, six months, or five years down the line. The actions you take now will be the vineyard that you will own months, years, and decades from now. This life is your field, your vineyard. Build the field and the life that you can and will be proud of. It is in your power."

LESSONS OF THE VINEYARD

DRINKING THE WINE, CELEBRATING WITH FAMILY AND FRIENDS

"You might say that it is too late, and you do not have the strength. You might say that you are too depressed and if no one cares about you, what is the point of even trying? Fast forward from the time I first visited Joseph. Michael calls me up sounding frantic:

"Benjamin, you will not believe this!"

"What? Are you okay?"

"I am great. It is about Joseph!"

"Oh no, what happened?"

"Joseph is engaged to be married!"

"What? Are you serious? That is amazing!"

"Yes, I just spoke with him and he said that he had been working on himself and he started to put himself out there more, meaning our Joseph began to have an interest in socializing more with people, which led to him meeting a woman. He did not tell either of us. He wanted to stay focused on taking action. He said that he followed the general ideas of Zehhu and the lessons of the vineyard that you both discussed and did his best to put them into action!"

Now Joseph the student has become the teacher."

Then I heard from Joseph himself and he had two requests from me.

The first was that I make sure I get to his wedding, rain, snow, or shine. The second was that I write down what we spoke about as best as

I can remember so that others battling the same monster of depression might benefit as well. The truth is that he did not have to make either of those requests because I would not miss Joseph's wedding for anything and I was so inspired by his own transformation that I wanted to write a book, at least to remind myself of everything that we spoke about so I could work harder to make the changes that Joseph did. But for others, I never thought about that until he mentioned it, so this book then was written to fulfill Joseph's request. Originally I wrote a version of this book which explained in detail how Joseph ended up in his state of depression. We thought this might be of use to anyone else who is facing similar adversities. But later I felt that the most important information for a person who wants to get out of the state of depression is how to cross the bridge from that state of a living death to a place of life despite the challenges of depression, not how any one of us might have ended up in the state of depression in the first place.

People end up in a state of depression for many different reasons, personal and/or biological. Our spotlight here is not why you or any other person becomes depressed; rather, our focus is on how to cross the bridge from depression to living. How to move on, how to cope more effectively with depression.

Therefore, instead of describing Joseph's descent into depression because of successive waves of trauma that he experienced over his life, we decided to immediately get into the concept of Zehhu, and the lessons of the vineyard, because anyone who is suffering from depression needs to know what to do now, urgently.

As I write this last chapter, I am 36,000 feet above the earth. I am flying back from Joseph's wedding to New York City. I said at the outset that I wanted to complete writing the conversations I had with Joseph before his wedding day and will make that promise as long as I add in "before his wedding day is over," for his wedding day is not yet over and by midnight tonight, I will be done and email him the first copy.

Before Joseph saw his beautiful bride for the first time, while he was putting on his tuxedo, he related to me his story, the way he would describe it:

"For a good ten years, I stewed heavily in the room of depression. I was isolated, catatonic much of the time, severely depressed, and saw no light at the end of the tunnel. I had little contact with family and/or friends. When I did meet people, I bled all over them, making them feel as bad as I did, and over time, they did not want to hear it anymore, just to protect their own selves and their own happiness. I can understand that today, as I know you do. For all of this time, I just replayed all the worst scenes and conversations that contributed to my flood of depression as you have described it, which drowned me out of most existence.

"I was so fortunate that you called me. I am grateful that Michael spoke for me and encouraged you to make contact with me. Personal attention matters. I did not think that anyone cared enough to physically show up at my apartment and see how I was doing. Nobody can know the results of all their actions and I myself had no clue that your call, visits, and our talks over the last few years would have any impact.

"I dismissed your ideas of the vineyard almost immediately, as being as an unorthodox treatment for depression as Zehhu, but it did strike a chord. I cannot explain why, but that one comparison of a person to a field, a vineyard, did make a difference as I sat in my room and visualized myself on the porch and looking out at rows and rows of vines stretching for miles. We all have the sights, scenes, sounds, and words that might inspire us. For years I heard many people tell me to let go, move on, drop the depression, just be happy, it will be okay. They all meant well, but none of those words penetrated my heart and mind.

"It was only after our discussions about the lessons of the vineyard that I began to think of the owner of the vineyard as you suggested, and how they would react if their vineyard was completely destroyed. Would they sit in the middle and mourn for the rest of their lives or would they rebuild?

"I answered in my own mind. The owner of the vineyard would rebuild. It is too beautiful not to rebuild. I started to believe that I too as the owner of my own field, my own life, could take action to rebuild. Not to put you down, Benjamin, but if you could make progress, I was sure that I could too!"

"You are so right and you did. Joseph is back!"

"During the last few years, I started to take small actions like cleaning up my room, my diet, my habits, and staying focused on small areas that I could control. I accepted that I couldn't control the thoughts and actions of other people.

"I accepted that whatever I thought they should be doing for me, I will start doing for myself.

"They should respect me? I should respect me. They should care about me? I should care about me. They should treat me better? I should treat me better, just like you said to me many times. I put all the shoulds on my shoulders and took responsibility for making anything and everything happen that might make me feel better. I accepted the idea that how I eat is a great start, because at least that is something directly under my control. I accepted that I have total control over what I eat, whether I exercise my body or not, and what I think, and those three areas can give me a big bang for the buck, and that I can realize a tremendous return on investment in the choices that I make in food, exercise, and thought.

"I started eating real food, walking whenever I could, doing whatever pushups I could, but did not do deadlifts and squats with barbells, just with dumbbells. I was embarrassed to go to a gym, so I bought a set of dumbbells and a bench and that was enough. Over the course of the last few years, even my battered body started to look fit. A year is not a long time considering all the years of damage and neglect that I had already put my body through. I am so grateful that my field, my body, has powers of rejuvenation and healing. I also made the investment of thinking differently. Instead of waiting for others to start liking me, I put that on my own shoulders. I took responsibility for starting to like myself, despite all the reasons I could come up with as to why I should hate myself."

"Hating yourself or your situation is one of the root causes of depression in my opinion, and is understandable in many cases. Why would anyone want to be depressed?

"Nobody wants to, but if you hate and despise yourself enough, if you hate your situation, if you think you are ugly or fat, if you think that your family hates you, your parents, kids, spouse, boss, whoever it might be, and especially if you hate yourself, I think that depression can be a result of beating yourself up without mercy. There is truly little that you can really control in your life. Think about it. You were born without your will or consent. You just showed up here one day and became aware that you exist.

"You continue to live, breathe, and exist, without your will or consent. You do not control the beating of your heart, the flow of your blood, and the chemical reactions within your own body. They all work on the subconscious level. You do not wake up and power up your body and brain, they just work, whether you tell them to or not. As much as we hope and try, at least at this time in history, we cannot control when our power shuts off, and when our life stops. So whoever thinks that they are in total control is not accurate. The only control that you have are what you eat, think, do, and the actions that you take with your hands, legs, eyes, ears, speech, and mind."

"Benjamin, at this point you know that you are preaching to the choir, right?"

"I am sorry, yes, I do know. You are only an hour away from taking vows to start your marriage, a new life, so awesome, please continue!"

"It is not really rocket science. All I did was take different and better actions. I am just a person who did not know how to deal with depression and who had no future in sight besides continuing to remain in my room of depression, obesity, and estrangement for the rest of my life.

"I had lost just about everything that mattered to me; family relationships, career, self-respect, my physical and mental health, and in a way, myself. I was so lost. Eating real food definitely started to help relieve me of the pounds of fat I was carrying. In turn, getting fitter helped me become more confident because I saw that there was an area in life where I did have control. I started to feel a little more optimistic about the future. I assume and hope that the medical professionals who had treated me over the years had my best interests at heart.

"Nevertheless, I cannot remember any doctor prescribing weightlifting and real food to fight my depression. And for sure no doctor was going to prescribe Zehhu and the lessons of the vineyard, but who knows, maybe someday in the future they will."

"I will take that as a compliment."

"I remember the Zoloft, Prozac, Neurontin, Effexor, Wellbutrin, Risperdal, Geodon, Lexapro, and Klonopin that I took and that were the source of countless negative side effects that had terrible consequences for my health, career, and most importantly, my children and family. My hope now is that you complete writing down all the main principles of Zehhu and the lessons of the vineyard to help other people the way this has helped me. That would be the best wedding present."

"I have been working on it for months now, since the day I found out from Michael that you were engaged."

"My hope is that someone who is looking for a way out of the malaise of depression might give some of the strategies a shot, find a few strength training exercises and real foods that they can stick with consistently, and watch the magic happen the way I have seen myself."

"My hope is that in the future, doctors will prescribe weightlifting, exercise, and nutrition first, before prescribing any medications at all. Of course there will be those that might only react well to certain medications, but there are other people like myself who can thrive on better food and movement. My dream is to create a non-profit organization called zehhu.org which will partner up people who are suffering from depression with certified trainers and/or nutritionists or meal plans and workouts to help fight their depression. Lift weights or lift your body weight and lift the quality of your food to fight depression."

"Finish the book first, Benjamin!"

"I am going to focus on the book. But wait a minute here. During all this time, how come you never told me or Michael that you were dating, that you had met a woman? We had so many conversations over the years and I had no clue that you were out in the world in that way. I knew you were walking, starting to run, working out, I saw the difference physically, but not once did you mention your soon-to-be wife."

"About a year and a half after I began to implement Zehhu and the lessons of the vineyard, I was a different person, both physically and the way I thought. The physical change was easy to see, a substantial weight loss of over fifty pounds. The change of thought was not visible, but it was real. I believed that there were actions that I could take, foods that I could eat, thoughts that I could think, that were all under my control and that could cause massive transformation in my life.

"Antidepressant medications are expensive and have numerous side effects. Hospitalization is not a cure; mainly it is done to protect a person if and when there is suicidal ideation or even worse, thoughts of hurting anyone else.

"Support groups are great but you have to find that desire within yourself to take that action that will help pull you out of the pit of depression. Depression is a serious issue with catastrophic consequences when not treated properly. For me it was the vineyard which I mocked that gave me the visualization that I needed to get started. For another person it might be something different. A picture is worth a thousand words and I think the same applies to a picture that you can hold in your mind, just as the vineyard was the picture of hope for me. I started to believe that life could get better.

"The notion that I could become healthy enough in body and mind to meet and fall in love with a woman ten years after the most painful period of my life was impossible for me to believe before we started talking. Soon after we met, I started to believe that this was real. I kept it to myself because I did not want people, even you or Michael, giving me opinions or comments. I also did not want to publicize something so good that was going on until we were actually engaged. I wanted to stay focused on our discussions, the lessons of the vineyard, because that is what helped me to get out of my depression and move forward. In fact, my fiancée told me that if she had met me just a few years ago, when you did, I would still be dreaming."

"Now I understand."

"But this marriage would never have happened without your ideas of Zehhu and the vineyard. This is a scene that I could not have imagined ten years ago but did start to imagine a few years ago as I began to focus on me.

"I started to feel more confident as I was eating better food and getting stronger. Every time I did squats with more weight, I felt that if I can handle this weight, then I can handle whatever situation I was in now. Every time I deadlifted more weight, I felt that just as I am lifting an amount of weight that I never thought possible, I can also lift myself out of the abyss that I was in. Every time I did another pushup, I felt that I could push through the pain of depression and estrangement. I had to create my own vineyard again. It had to be different from the vineyard I had before the storm, but I can and must make every effort possible to rebuild as long as I own my field, my body and mind. By the way, Benjamin, I have some of my own suggestions after spending the last few years thinking about the lessons of the vineyard. Do you mind?"

"Go for it. I am sure that there are many more lessons that I have not thought about that are waiting to be revealed."

"When selling wine, a precious drink for thousands of years, it is natural to place the wine in the best packaging possible. Similarly, as you work on yourself both physically and with your thoughts, the more you present yourself to the world, and more importantly yourself, the more attractive your wine will be for all. This must start with you. Like everything else the vineyard teaches us, you must market yourself to yourself first. How? Take care of yourself! This is not rocket science, but to a person that has lived in depression and just did not care about anything, it can be a new and even challenging task. Take better care of yourself from the clothing you wear to brushing your teeth. Do your best to be the best version of yourself possible.

"Celebrate the small wins; the additional pushup, the added weight to the bar when you are doing deadlifts, the extra mile that you ran, meeting your goal weight, body fat percentage, or cholesterol level. Every time you meet a new goal, you are improving, being productive and getting better. The overall goal is to celebrate life, the amazing potential that life has to give joy to us and to those that know and care about us, and the great potential that we have to help others.

"This is the intention of the owner of the vineyard as well. The customers pay for their wine in some cases and the vineyard might give away their wine in other cases, but no matter what, creating that beautiful vineyard and wine is a labor of love. Apply that same labor of love to your own life. Accept who you are and where you are right now and start to work on lifting yourself up out of depression and into a new world of gradually rebuilding your life.

"Any person who is struggling with depression right now might be pleasantly surprised as I have been at the results. Those are the people that you and I want to help. A person might have experienced great loss, but now is the time to start focusing on how to experience gain, and create a new life.

"We will always carry the wounds of the past, but they can be kept in the archives and now is the time to open up a new chapter in life, one where it is okay to be happy and celebrate. This is exactly where I strive to be today; celebrating a new life. The purpose of the owner's vineyard is to ultimately produce great wine that can be enjoyed by friends and family together; so too we must begin to enjoy life again.

"There is potential guilt and conflict enjoying life after having lived in depression for so many years, but my experience teaches that when you are in the middle of creating a new field, it is possible, as long as you keep the focus on your new life, the new field that you are creating."

"That was awesome!"

"It is time for me to go. Time to move on to a new chapter in life, time to celebrate!"

"Benjamin, will you hold the ring for me?"

"Yes Joseph, of course, thank you!"

"Thank you for everything my friend, see you inside!"

"Congratulations, Joseph! We are all so glad that you are back, that you have crossed the bridge from depression to life!"

"Anyone suffering with depression can start to help themselves with good nutrition and exercise. Finish writing everything down Benjamin; anyone suffering with depression can potentially start to help themselves with good nutrition and exercise. Plus I want to be able to review the ideas myself. I was the first to say that Zehhu and the vineyard are unusual ideas, that better thoughts, better food and pushups will not make a difference, but look who is so wrong, me, the groom, and I am so happy to have been so wrong!"

Joseph finished putting on his tuxedo and started walking toward his beautiful bride. I had tears in my eyes. There were many other well-wishers there at Joseph's wedding, including Joseph's children, who walked him down the aisle. To say it was a moving and special day is an understatement.

This was the intention of the owner of the vineyard from the beginning; to create wine that will gladden the hearts of others and him. Living with that mindset creates energy of living with clear and optimistic goals in mind and we should celebrate every achievement.

It is my sincere desire that if you are suffering from depression today, these words in *Zehhu: Crossing the Bridge from Depression to Life* will help to inspire you to build a new vineyard for yourself and that very soon, you will celebrate together with your family and friends, drinking the new wine you have created and celebrating your new life. When the celebration begins, please do not forget to invite us!